Graceful Beginnings
Short and Easy for Anyone New to the Bible

Seek the Treasure

Unearthing the riches of Christ in Ephesians

MELANIE NEWTON

JOYFUL
WALK
BIBLE
STUDIES

We express our thanks to Heather Newton and Aimee Jones who served as editors for this study.

Seek the Treasure: Unearthing the Riches of Christ in Ephesians

© 2025 by Melanie Newton. All rights reserved.

Published by Joyful Walk Press. Flower Mound, TX.

ISBN: 979-8-9925750-7-1

For questions about the use of this study guide or for bulk orders, please email us at melanienewton.com/contact.

Cover graphic, "COLOURBOX5894918.jpg, was purchased from colourbox.com, used by permission. Other graphics in the lessons are adapted from public domain images.

Melanie Newton is the author of "Graceful Beginnings" books for anyone new to the Bible and "Joyful Walk Bible Studies" for established Christians. Her mission is to help women learn to study the Bible for themselves and to grow their Bible-teaching skills to lead others.

Joyful Walk Bible Studies are grace-based studies for women of all ages. Each study guide follows the inductive method of Bible study (observation, interpretation, application) in a warm and inviting format.

We pray that you will find *Seek the Treasure* to be a resource that God will use to strengthen you in your faith walk with Him.

Christ-Focused • Grace-Based • Bible-Rich

JOYFUL WALK PRESS
Flower Mound, TX

MELANIE NEWTON

Melanie Newton is a Louisiana girl who made the choice to follow Jesus while attending LSU. She and her husband Ron married and moved to Texas for him to attend Dallas Theological Seminary. They stayed in Texas where Ron led a wilderness camping ministry for troubled youth for many years. Ron now helps corporations with their challenging employees and is the author of the top-rated business book, *No Jerks on the Job*.

Melanie jumped into raising three Texas-born children and serving in ministry to women at her church. Through the years, the Lord has given her opportunity to do Bible teaching and to write grace-based Bible studies for women that are now available from her website (melanienewton.com) and on Bible.org. *Graceful Beginnings* books are for anyone new to the Bible. *Joyful Walk Bible Studies* are for maturing Christians.

Melanie Newton loves to help women learn how to study the Bible for themselves. She also teaches online courses for women to grow their Bible-teaching skills to help others—all with the goal of getting to know Jesus more along the way. Her heart's desire is to encourage you to have a joyful relationship with Jesus Christ so you are willing to share that experience with others around you.

"Jesus took hold of me in 1972, and I've been on this great adventure ever since. My life is a gift of God, full of blessings in the midst of difficult challenges. The more I've learned and experienced God's absolutely amazing grace, the more I've discovered my faith walk to be a joyful one. I'm still seeking that joyful walk every day..."

Melanie

OTHER BIBLE STUDIES BY MELANIE NEWTON

Graceful Beginnings Series books for anyone new to the Bible:
A Fresh Start (basics for new Christians)
Painting the Portrait of Jesus (the Gospel of John)
The God You Can Know (the character of God)
Grace Overflowing (an overview of Paul's 13 letters)
The Walk from Fear to Faith (7 Old Testament women)
Satisfied by His Love (women who knew Jesus)
Seek the Treasure (study of Ephesians)
Pathways to a Joyful Walk (6 pathways to a joy-filled life)s

Joyful Walk Bible Studies for growing Christians:
Adorn Yourself with Godliness (1 Timothy and Titus +Spanish)
Everyday Women, Ever Faithful God (Old Testament women +Spanish)
Connecting Faith to Life on Planet Earth (Genesis 1-11; Revelation)
Graceful Living (the essentials for a grace-based Christian life)
Graceful Living Today (a devotional journal for a joyful life)
Healthy Living (Colossians and Philemon)
Heartbreak to Hope (the Gospel of Mark)
Identity: Sticking to Your Faith in a Pull-Apart World (Ezra - Malachi)
Knowing Jesus, Knowing Joy (Philippians +Spanish)
Live Out His Love (New Testament women)
Perspective (1and 2 Thessalonians)
Profiles of Perseverance (Old Testament men +Spanish)
Radical Acts (Acts)
Reboot, Renew, Rejoice (1 and 2 Chronicles)
The God-Dependent Woman (2 Corinthians)
To Be Found Faithful (2 Timothy)

Resources for leading others
Be a Christ-Focused Small Group Leader
Leap into Lifestyle Disciplemaking
Bible Study Leadership Made Easy (online video course)
Painting the Picture of Jesus (the "I Am's" of Jesus lessons)
Teaching Children the God They Can Know (the character of God)
Download our catalogue and get resources for your spiritual growth at melanienewton.com.

Contents

Introduction.. 1

1: The Treasure of Jesus Christ.. 7

2: The Treasure of Your Rescue from Darkness.................... 21

3: The Treasure of Every Spiritual Blessing in Christ........... 33

4: The Treasure of Being Dearly Loved 43

5: The Treasure of the Church 55

6: The Treasure of God's Empowering Presence.................. 69

7: The Treasure of Godliness 83

8: The Treasure of Victory in Christ.................................... 97

The Biblical Process for Dealing with Recognized Sin........109

The Holy Spirit's Empowering Presence...............................110

Sources 113

Introduction

GRACEFUL BEGINNINGS

The *Graceful Beginnings* books are Bible studies specifically designed for anyone new to the Bible—whether you are a new Christian or you just feel insecure about understanding the Bible. The short and easy lessons will introduce you to your God and His way of approaching life in simple terms that can be easily understood.

Just as a newborn baby needs to know the love and trustworthiness of her parents, the new Christian needs to know and experience the love and trustworthiness of her God. *A Fresh Start* is the first book in the series, laying a good foundation of truth for you to grasp and apply to your life. The other books in the series can be done in any order although we do make suggestions at the end of each book regarding what to study next.

SOME BIBLE BASICS

Throughout these lessons, you will use a Bible to answer questions as you discover treasure about your life with Christ. The Bible is one book containing a collection of 66 books combined together for our benefit. It is divided into two main parts: Old Testament and New Testament.

The Old Testament tells the story of the beginning of the world and God's promises to mankind given through the nation of Israel. It tells how the people of Israel obeyed and disobeyed God over many, many years. All the stories and messages in the Old Testament lead up to Jesus Christ's coming to the earth.

The New Testament tells the story of Jesus Christ, the early Christians, and God's promises to all those who believe in Jesus. You can think of the Old Testament as "before Christ" and the New Testament as "after Christ."

Each book of the Bible is divided into chapters and verses within those chapters to make it easier to study. Bible references include the book name, chapter number and verse number(s). For example, Ephesians 2:8 refers to the New Testament book of Ephesians, the 2nd chapter, and verse 8 within that 2nd chapter. Printed Bibles have a "Table of Contents" in the front to help you locate books by page number. Bible apps also have a contents list by book and chapter.

The Bible verses highlighted at the beginning of each lesson in this study are from the New International Version® (NIV®) unless otherwise indicated. You can use any version of the Bible to answer the questions, but using an easy-to-read translation (CSB, NLT, NET, ESV) will help you gain confidence in understanding what you are reading. You can find all these translations in the "YouVersion App" or on biblegateway.com.

This study capitalizes certain pronouns referring to God, Jesus and the Holy Spirit—He, Him, His, Himself—just to make the reading of the study information less confusing. Some Bible translations likewise capitalize those pronouns referring to God; others do not. It is simply a matter of preference, not a requirement.

NEW TESTAMENT SUMMARY

The New Testament opens with the births of John the Baptist and Jesus. About 30 years later, John challenged the Jews to indicate their repentance (turning from sin and toward God) by submitting to water baptism—a familiar Old Testament practice used for repentance as well as when a non-Jew (often called Gentiles) converted to Judaism (to be washed clean of idolatry).

Jesus, who is also known by the title "Christ," is God's Son, fully God and fully man. Jesus publicly showed the world what God is like and taught His perfect ways for 3 – 3½ years. After preparing 12 disciples to continue Christ's earthly work, He died voluntarily on a cross for mankind's sin, rose from the dead, and returned to Heaven. The account of His earthly life is recorded in 4 books known as the Gospels (the biblical books of Matthew, Mark, Luke and John named after the compiler of each account).

After Jesus' return to Heaven, the followers of Christ were then empowered by the Holy Spirit and spread God's salvation message among the Jews, a number of whom believed in Christ. The apostle Paul and others carried the good news to the Gentiles during 3 missionary journeys (much of this recorded in the book of Acts). Paul wrote 13 New Testament letters to churches & individuals (Romans through Philemon). The section in our Bible from Hebrews to Jude contains 8 additional letters penned by five men, including two apostles (Peter and John) and two of Jesus' half-brothers (James and Jude, whose mother was Mary). The author of Hebrews is unknown. The apostle John also recorded Revelation, which summarizes God's final program for the world. The Bible ends as it began—with a new, sinless creation.

ELEMENTS OF EACH LESSON

This book covers Paul's letter known as "Ephesians." It is a short and easy study covering the basic information that you need to know as a believer in Christ.

1. Each lesson begins with a Bible verse that relates to the focus of the lesson and a prayer. Prayer is just talking to God as conversation with someone who loves you dearly. The beginning prayer simply asks Jesus to teach you through the lesson.

2. This is followed by a simple study of the passage being covered by the lesson. Read the Bible verses and answer the associated questions. This study uses the NIV translation. We recommend you use that or other easy-to-read translations (CSB, NLT, NET, ESV). See "Bible Basics" above for online sources of these.

3. In the "Your Treasure in Christ" section at the end of the study questions, you will be encouraged to dwell more on what you learned in the lesson that applies to your life today.

4. A short teaching session ("Seek the Treasure") follows each lesson giving additional insight into the verses covered by the lesson plus application. Find podcasts for these lessons at melanienewton.com/podcasts (choose "16: Ephesians) and on most podcast providers. Or you can read the blogs associated with the podcasts at melanienewton.com/blog. Choose Ephesians category then scroll to find the title you want. Listen to the first podcast as an introduction to the study.

5. Every "Seek the Treasure" section is followed by a "Reflect" time for you to respond to what you learned and a prayer of trust that Jesus will help you recognize anything that you are substituting for Him.

SMALL GROUP DISCUSSION

While you can work through these lessons as a personal study, this topic is perfect to use for small groups. Share the following suggested guidelines with the group members to maximize your discussion group experience.

➢   Set aside some time each week to do the study questions so that you will get to know God better.

- Consistently attend whether your lesson is done or not. You will learn from the discussion.

- Respect each other's insights. Listen thoughtfully. Share your own insights, but do not dominate the discussion.

- Celebrate unity in Christ by avoiding controversial subjects such as politics, divisive issues and denominational differences.

- Maintain confidentiality of whatever is shared within the group.

Enjoy your small group discussion and learn from one another. As you journal parts of your story and share that with your group members, you will have a greater connection with each other. And you'll have more reason to praise our ever-faithful God as you see and hear how He has been faithful to each of you through the years. A small group is a great place to share how you are seeking the treasure of Christ in your life. Discussing the lesson and the teaching session should take about an hour, making this an easy study to fit into a busy workday schedule.

Suggested Leader Guide for Group Discussion:

Go to my website, melanienewton.com/ephesians-study to download a more detailed discussion guide for this study. Or follow the suggestions below:

1. Pray for the Holy Spirit to teach you what He wants you to know through the lesson.

2. Work through the LESSON together, reading the Bible verses and discussing the questions. Predetermine which of the explanatory paragraphs you will read as a group.

3. Read the "YOUR TREASURE IN CHRIST" summary and share responses to any included application questions.

5. Discuss parts of the "SEEK THE TREASURE" section that you want to emphasize. Or listen to the podcast together. REFLECT on the teaching.

6. Pray for the group members – ask Jesus to satisfy your hearts through knowing Him. Thank God for His grace toward you and His love for you.

7. Remind each person to do the next lesson and listen to the related podcast before the group meets again.

SEEK THE TREASURE

Do you have a special little box or shelf that contains personal treasures that are important to who you are? We all love the idea of some kind of treasure in a treasure chest.

Humans seek anything that will satisfy the spiritual hunger in our souls and "guarantee" successful living. God intended that hunger to be filled with Himself. Yet, instead of relying on God, we shop around at different sources to see what we want to put in our treasure chest. Will it work to make me lucky? Or solve my problem? Or make my soul happy?

There are so many things out there on the internet or in social media that we can try. We look for the latest thing that guarantees success at … whatever. Then, we go for it. These can be powerful influences on us as women, but they are substitutes for the real thing.

Everything that we already have in Christ is more powerful and valuable for successful living than any of those substitutes. The problem is that we have to recognize that substitute treasure is worthless. We will be unearthing the riches of Christ throughout our study of Ephesians. Our God offers us the most wonderful treasure we could ever want—by faith in Christ.

Let Jesus satisfy your heart with the confidence that the treasure you have in Him is more powerful and valuable than anything you could substitute for Him.

It's going to be a great journey. And I'm so glad to be walking beside you!

Melanie Newton

The Treasure of Jesus Christ

"That power is the same as the mighty strength [God] exerted when He raised Christ from the dead and seated Him at His right hand in the heavenly realms, far above all rule and authority, power and dominion, and every name that is invoked, not only in the present age but also in the one to come." (Ephesians 1:19-21, NIV)

> **Recommended:** Listen to the podcast "WHAT IS IN YOUR TREASURE CHEST?" before doing this lesson to get some background for the whole study. Use the following listener guide. Some of the information is also included in the lesson itself.

Two thousand years ago, God took in a rebel named Paul, gave him the treasure of Himself and sent him out to invite others to receive that treasure, also. Some of those who responded lived in the region of Ephesus on the west coast of modern Turkey. The letter we'll be studying together was originally written by Paul to those Ephesians.

The Ephesians and their treasure chest

Two words described Ephesus—**prominent** and **obsessed**. Ephesus was a prominent city along major highways, commercially prosperous, and had a large population of at least ¼ million people. And Ephesus was a city obsessed with the supernatural, especially the power of evil spirits that could make life miserable. The people tried anything that would defeat the enemy and guarantee a "successful" life.

Prominent and obsessed are both related to power. For the Ephesians, life was all about power. Who or what had the most power? And their identity came from their power sources. That was reflected in their treasure chests. They had magic formulas, self-help scrolls, and figurines of their superhero goddess named Artemis. Those things were what the Ephesians had in their treasure chests, often kept in a secret place in their houses. They thought all that was powerful enough and valuable enough to satisfy their spiritual needs.

Then, God introduced them to Jesus Christ through Paul. They soon found out that their own treasure chests were worthless compared to what God offered them.

Seeking treasure for our treasure chests today

Humans today are still fascinated by treasure-seeking. People spend millions of dollars seeking legendary treasure, and we watch as they do it.

> ➢ We seek today to fill our personal treasure chests with whatever will make us successful in life but are told there's no devil, no supernatural, and no need for God because science will find the answer to everything.

> ➢ Yet, we are drawn to supernatural power, though not necessarily God's power. At its core, this is seeking anything to satisfy the spiritual hunger in our souls and "guarantee" successful living.

> ➢ God intended that hunger to be filled with Himself. Yet, instead of relying on God, we shop around at different sources to see what we want to put in our treasure chest.

We look for the latest thing that guarantees success at … whatever. Then, we go for it. These can be powerful influences on us as women, but they are substitutes for the real thing.

Your heart will be where your treasure is.

> *"Don't store up treasures here on earth, where moths eat them and rust destroys them, and where thieves break in and steal. Store your treasures in heaven, where moths and rust cannot destroy, and thieves do not break in and steal. Wherever your treasure is, there the desires of your heart will also be." (Matthew 6:19-21, NLT)*

Where your treasure is, that's where the desires of your heart will be. Dear believer, what are you relying on for success in your life?

Everything that we already have in Christ is more powerful and valuable for successful living than any of those substitutes. The problem is this: We have to recognize that **substitute** treasure is **worthless**. Together, as we study Ephesians, we will learn how to recognize substitute treasure and see that our God offers us the most wonderful treasure we could ever want in Christ.

Let Jesus satisfy your heart with the confidence that the treasure you have in Him is more powerful and valuable than anything you could substitute for Him.

THE ABC'S OF EPHESIANS — AUTHOR, BACKGROUND, AND CONTEXT

Like any book you read, it always helps to know a bit about the author, the background setting for the story, and where the book fits into a series (its context). The same is true of Bible books.

Author

A man named Paul authored the letter we know as Ephesians. He lived at the same time as Jesus and for many years afterwards. But we have no indication that he ever met Jesus before the Resurrection. Paul was a well-educated, devout Jew. Jews believed in the one true God and followed the Mosaic Law, which was God's law for them.

In the Bible, he is known by two names: his Hebrew name "Saul" and his Roman name "Paul." To keep things simple, we will call him by his Roman name because that's what he mainly used in his travels and ministry.

At first, Paul didn't believe Jesus was the Son of God and fought against Christians, dragging them out of their homes and putting them in prison. He was determined to wipe out all the Christians. Then, one day, Jesus appeared to him and grabbed his attention. After believing in Jesus Christ as his Savior, Paul was sent by Jesus to take the gospel to the people who were not Jews, those called Gentiles in the Bible.

Paul took "missionary journeys" to many cities in the Roman Empire. Wherever Paul and his co-workers visited, people heard the message about Jesus and became Christians. The new believers met together and formed a church in that city. Paul loved those people very much and wanted to hear how the young churches were doing. Someone would bring him news about the church members in a particular city. Then, Paul would write them a letter, usually answering some questions they had or teaching them something they needed to know about living as Christians.

The Holy Spirit guided Paul to write those letters and preserved 13 of them for us to have in our Bibles. In fact, Paul authored more of the New Testament writings than anyone else. These letters are a gift to us 2000 years later.

Background

On his third missionary journey, Paul went to the large city of Ephesus. The Ephesians were obsessed with power, especially the use of magic. They were very afraid of evil spirits and bad luck so they clung to anything that would keep them safe. That included magic words written on socks or recited aloud to chase evil spirits away, necklaces with magic power to give them luck when playing sports, and books of magic spells to use for protection. So Paul spent three years with the Ephesians, teaching classes every day to those who wanted to learn a new way to live. Many became Christians and gave up their old way of life.

A few years later, on a visit to Jerusalem, Paul was falsely accused and arrested. After a long time of waiting to be released, he finally appealed to Caesar and was sent to Rome. That's where Paul was when he wrote this letter—imprisoned in Rome, chained to a Roman soldier 24/7. But he was given the freedom to have visitors and write letters, including this letter to the Ephesians.

The letter to the Ephesians was written about 4-5 years after Paul left Ephesus. Before his arrest, Paul had met briefly with the Ephesian church leaders in a nearby city to give them words of encouragement. He received news about the church from various sources. But he had not been back to Ephesus.

Context

The letter to the Ephesians is one of four letters Paul wrote from his Roman imprisonment that the Holy Spirit chose to preserve in our New Testaments. The others are the letters to the Philippians in northern Greece, to the Colossians in central Turkey, and to Philemon who was a leader in the Colossian church.

The order in which we find Paul's letters in the New Testament is not based on chronology but mostly on size. Ephesians is found after Galatians which was written more than 10 years earlier. Philippians and Colossians follow. But Philemon, the shortest letter, is found at the end of Paul's letters.

EPHESUS AND ITS TREASURE CHEST

As we mentioned earlier, two words described Ephesus—prominent and obsessed. The city was prominent because of its location along major highways, its commercial prosperity, and its large population of ¼ million people. It also had impressive buildings, including the Roman governor's office.

Ephesians were obsessed with the supernatural, especially the power of evil spirits that could make their lives miserable. The city was filled with magicians, psychics, and astrologers. The people tried anything that would defeat the enemy and guarantee a "successful" life.

Prominent and obsessed are both related to power. For the Ephesians, life was all about power. Who or what had the most power? And their identity came from their power sources. That was reflected in their treasure chests. That is true for us as well.

GOD'S TREASURE FOR THEM AND FOR US

Paul taught the Ephesians that Jesus Christ was the Son of God who came to earth to live as a human, died for their sins, and was resurrected from the dead to give them new life. Paul's message everywhere was consistently the same. "Believe in the Lord Jesus Christ, and you will be saved."

Paul started as usual in the synagogue preaching to Jews and interested Gentiles. Some of the synagogue leaders put a stop to that. So Paul took the new Christians with him and began daily teaching sessions in a local lecture hall for the next two years. The book of Acts describes this time.

Read Acts 19:8-12.

How effective and far-reaching was Paul's teaching in Ephesus (verse 10)?

The Ephesians' concept of power was that of an impersonal substance one could use to one's own advantage. What did God do through Paul to get their attention on Him instead (verses 11-12)?

Miracles are already amazing, but God did more than usual. The Greek word translated "extraordinary" means "to hit the mark like one who is throwing a javelin or arrow." God was targeting their need for spiritual power with "extra-miraculous" miracles. God showed them that He was **more powerful** than their magicians, lucky charms, and magic words. God was more powerful than the evil spirits or any substitute they might trust for protection against evil. God knew what they really needed— Himself!

> *Our very creative God knows how to use His power to target your spiritual need as well. How has God targeted your need and drawn you closer to Him?*

Read Acts 19:13-20.

Invoking names to control evil spirits was a form of magic practiced in Ephesus. The practice had been taken up even by Jews.

> *When the news about the magicians who tried to imitate Paul became known, what happened (verse 17)?*

> *What did the new believers in Christ do (verses 18-19)?*

> *What was the result (verse 20)?*

Many Ephesians trusted in Jesus for their protection, so they got rid of their substitutes. They had a big bonfire to burn their sorcerer's manuals, lucky socks, and magic necklaces. They attended Paul's classes then spread out and shared the good news about Jesus throughout western Turkey, establishing churches all over the place. The letter to the Ephesians was written to the church in Ephesus and to the churches in the surrounding area. The Holy Spirit guided the writing of this letter so it is a gift from God to us. Let's dig into it.

Read Ephesians 1:1-2.

As mentioned in the ABC's of Ephesians, Paul wrote this letter to the Christians living in Ephesus about 4-5 years after he had last seen them.

Read Ephesians 3:1 and 3:8.

What does Paul say about himself (verse 1)?

What was his mission from God (verse 8)?

Paul knew he was a prisoner of Rome, but he considered himself a prisoner of Christ in whom he had entrusted his life.

THE POWER OF JESUS CHRIST

As you study Ephesians, you will see that Paul reminded them, and us, that no matter how hard life gets, Jesus Christ is still more powerful than any substitute "good luck charm." And Christ's power makes it possible for us to live God's way today and not be afraid.

Let's find out how powerful Christ is and how His power works for us.

Read Ephesians 1:19-23.

In verses 19-20, what does Paul want the Ephesians to know about the might of God's power?

Where is Christ (verse 20)?

Over what does He have authority (verse 21)?

Over what else does He have authority (verse 22)?

What is meant by "all rule and authority, power and dominion" in verse 21? That phrase includes all spiritual powers—the good angels, the demons, and Satan himself. We've mentioned evil spirits in this lesson so far, but we really haven't answered the question, "Who are they?"

Evil spirits are demons. They are angels created at the beginning of creation. The Bible teaches that one angel rebelled against God and took 1/3 of the angels with him. We know that rebel leader as Satan, also called "the devil," and those with him in rebellion against God as "demons." Satan and his demonic forces do everything they can to thwart the good purposes of God—gaining control over people through deception, counterfeits, fear, manipulation, and torment.

In His life on earth, Jesus as the Son of God demonstrated that He had greater power over all the spirit world—the good angels who served Him plus Satan and his demonic forces. The resurrected Jesus, in heaven once again, is still more powerful than Satan and any demon. Jesus Christ has the power of a great king who is king above all other powers and kings.

"Every title that can be given" refers to those names used in magical formulas to control evil spirits as you saw in Acts 19:13. Demons were behind every reference to evil spirits.

Read Ephesians 2:6.

Where does God place us as believers?

In the mind and plan of God, all Christians are seated with Christ in heaven under His powerful authority. Notice that we are not under Christ's feet like all the angelic powers. We are seated within His authority over anything that could come against us.

People in a western culture don't consciously admit to being afraid of evil spirits like the Ephesians were and like some parts of our world still are. But we do fear bad things happening and try to manage supernatural or cosmic power in such a way that results are "virtually guaranteed" in our favor. As a culture, and really as humans everywhere, we seek anything that will satisfy the spiritual hunger in our souls and "guarantee" successful living.

What are your substitute powers?

Do you possess anything that you think gives you good luck— special socks, a bead necklace, or a rabbit's foot? Why do you think that item has power to give you good luck?

Some things are associated with causing bad luck—walking under a ladder, breaking a mirror, or jinxing a pitcher throwing a no-hitter. But do you think those things really have power to give you or others bad luck?

Those are substitute treasures. The most powerful treasure we could ever have is Jesus Christ. *We have no need for any substitutes to keep bad things from happening to us.* We don't need lucky socks, magic words, or special charms to make sure good things happen to us. Substitute treasure is worthless.

YOUR TREASURE IN CHRIST

What do you tend to rely upon in order to be "successful" in life or to defeat any perceived "enemies?" Self-sufficiency? Academic degree? Social status? What else?

Are you willing to learn how to get rid of your substitutes and cling to your treasure in Christ alone? Why or why not?

Through Paul's message to the Ephesians, our God is saying to you and me, "Why trust in any substitute power to help you live a good life?" Nothing is as powerful as Jesus Christ Himself. His power is available to every believer through His Spirit living inside you.

Christ wants you to get rid of those substitutes in your head as well as in your heart and your experiences. You can say to Him, *"My treasure in you, Lord Jesus, is more powerful and valuable than anything I could substitute for You. Please confirm that in my heart."*

SEEK YOUR TREASURE IN JESUS CHRIST

SEEK THE TREASURE

Recommended: *Listen to the podcast "SEEK THE TREASURE OF JESUS CHRIST." Use the section below as a listener guide.*

As Paul taught the Ephesians about Jesus, God validated Paul's words by doing miracles through him. Miracles in the Bible (1) authenticate the message and the messenger. They also (2) demonstrate God's compassion for women, men, and children. And miracles (3) show that God's power is beyond that of any human as well as Satan and his demonic forces. God knew that the Ephesians believed in supernatural power. They were just seeking the wrong ones. So God did extra-miraculous miracles that targeted their need, drawing their attention to His Son, Jesus Christ. He does the same for us.

Christianity is Christ! It is not a lifestyle. It's not rules of conduct. It's not a society of people who are joined together by the sprinkling or covering of water. Christianity is a relationship with the Lord Jesus Christ. And Jesus invites every man, woman, and child into a close relationship with Himself as brothers, sisters, and friends.

But who is Jesus? The New Testament teaches that He is the Son of God who died for our sins and rose again so that we could have eternal life just by believing in Him as the Savior—fully God and fully man.

Jesus is fully God.

Jesus claimed to be fully God and demonstrated it through His life and His words. That is clearly seen in the text of the first four books of the New Testament which tell of Jesus' life.

Jesus not only claimed to be God, but He also claimed to be the answer to the needs of the human heart as God would. Jesus consistently called God His father. He declared His right to judge and said that He deserves the honor that belongs to God. The works He was doing could only be done by God. He clearly and boldly claimed His identity as the promised anointed one of God. He claimed to be the Son of Man who was also the Son of God. Those are all radical statements.

All God's powers and attributes are in Jesus. There is nothing missing. There is nothing more of God that we can get apart from Jesus (Colossians 1:19).

In the New Testament, Jesus is called the **Lord** Jesus Christ. Christ is His title. It comes from the Greek word *christos,* which translates the Hebrew title "Messiah" meaning "anointed one." According to Psalm 110:1, the Messiah would sit at the right hand of God and be called Lord. Jesus claimed this for Himself. Jesus is the Son of God who is Christ the Lord.

Jesus is fully human.

Jesus is also fully human. We have a harder time wrapping our brains around **that** fact than we do believing He was God. Yet, Jesus experienced the normal process of body development from a child to an adult man. He obeyed His parents and learned to live with at least 4 brothers and 2 sisters (Mark 6:3).

In His human body, Jesus felt hunger and thirst. Tears fell down His cheeks when His friends were hurting. He had the normal human response of anger against the stubborn hearts of the religious people who opposed Him and were not teachable. During the last hours before His death, He experienced distress and pain just as you would.

And because Jesus was fully human, He understands every single one of your heartaches. He experienced human life for more than 30 years. He gets your physical pain, your feelings of rejection, and your strained relationships. He gets your abuse, your grief, and your impatience because those were part of His life as well.

Jesus also demonstrated in His life on earth how much He loved and valued women. He taught them truth about God, forgave them for their sins, accepted them in His circle of followers, and gave new life to them after His resurrection. His care for them was so countercultural to what they had previously known. Women recognized that and responded with love for Him and a desire to serve Him. He does the same for you today.

Jesus was fully human and lived as a human, but He did not sin. Why is that? He lived in perfect love for God the Father, His Father. Because He loved God perfectly, He lived in perfect dependence on God the Father and perfect obedience. And He gave us a pattern to follow so that we can learn to love God and to depend upon Him and obey Him by faith too.

Jesus was completely human while being completely God. None of us can really understand how this is, but we must accept it as truth. His death on the cross and His resurrection from the dead provided everything you needed to have a relationship with God and satisfying spiritual life.

When Christians lose confidence in God

We can know all this about Christ to be true. But then life's challenges hit us squarely in the face. What happens when you get tired of waiting for God to answer your prayer? What happens when you don't see Him rescuing you from a tough situation? What happens when He doesn't heal your disease? When you lose confidence in God's power to manage whatever is burdening you, where are you tempted to turn?

When Christians lose confidence in the one true God to meet our needs, we look for something that will work, such as formulas for "success," religious experiences, and lucky practices. We saw that happening in Ephesus in Acts 19:13-16. Those verses tell us two things: 1) demons are real and dangerous forces and 2) the spiritualism of the culture invaded even Judaism. Those Jews had turned to using an acceptable practice in their culture to bring about success in their work—relying on substitute powers rather than on God.

This is really a very sad passage because it hits close to home. Whenever Christians lose confidence in the one true God to meet our needs, we begin to rely on the aid of other powers, even subconsciously. This is evidenced by what we do and say, even by what we post on Facebook and other social media.

> ➤ What picture do you post on social media, claiming that it is the answer for the day's stressful challenges? That's a substitute power.

> ➤ Do you do anything to avoid "bad luck" or to guarantee "good luck?" Those are substitute powers.

> ➤ Do you follow a certain formula for prayer guaranteeing that God hears you and will answer your prayer? The formula becomes the substitute. Not using it might make you feel like you can't pray.

> ➤ Do you follow a certain procedure to get on a higher level with God and expect to hear His voice audibly every time you pray? The procedure becomes the substitute for submission to the authority of Christ.

When you recognize your use of substitutes, remember what the Ephesians did in Acts 19. They burned it up! They deleted it from daily life. They saw that the treasure they had in Jesus was more powerful than any of their substitutes. So they were willing to get rid of their substitutes and cling to their treasure in Christ alone.

Jesus Christ is fully powerful.

Jesus is your treasure and your power source to overcome anything you picture coming against you. In fact, the Greek word for power, *dunamis,* is where we get our word dynamite and is often translated as "miracles" in the New Testament. And Paul used the word, *dunamis,* seven times in this short letter to refer to the power of God available to every believer to meet every need. God's dynamite power is **for** us and **within** us.

Jesus Christ is over everything. Evil is under His feet. As we sit with Him in heaven, evil is under our feet. All we have to do is remember our place with Him. So picture yourself sitting with Jesus in the heavenly realms, with your treasure chest containing all the wonderful blessings you get from Him. It's not about something you do. It's something that has already been done and given to you by faith in Christ. You can rest in that and all the treasure that comes with it. That's the way to guarantee successful living—God's way of successful living. You can trust in that!

Let Jesus satisfy your heart with the confidence that the treasure you have in Him is more powerful and valuable than anything you could substitute for Him.

Reflect

Read the words to this beautiful worship song. Then, respond to God with the prayer prompts given in the box below.

Death could not hold You, The veil tore before You, You silence the boast of sin and grave. The heavens are roaring, The praise of Your glory, For You are raised to life again. You have no rival, You have no equal, Now and forever, God You reign. Yours is the kingdom, Yours is the glory, Yours is the Name above all names What a powerful Name it is, What a powerful Name it is, The Name of Jesus Christ my King. What a powerful Name it is, Nothing can stand against. What a powerful Name it is, The Name of Jesus.
("What A Beautiful Name" by Ben Fielding & Brooke Ligertwood)

Pray: Thank God for the treasure He has given you in Jesus Christ. Ask Him to help you recognize anything that you are substituting for Him. Ask Him to help you trust in Him alone for the power to be "successful" in life.

The Treasure of Your Rescue from Darkness

"But because of his great love for us, God, who is rich in mercy, made us alive with Christ even when we were dead in transgressions—it is by grace you have been saved." (Ephesians 2:4-5, NIV)

Pray: Lord Jesus, please teach me through this lesson.

Ephesus was a prominent city because of its size and location. It was also a place obsessed with the supernatural, especially the power of evil spirits. The people of Ephesus tried anything that would defeat the enemy and guarantee a "successful" life. The words "prominent" and "obsessed" are both related to power. For the Ephesians, life was all about power. Who or what had the most power?

So God targeted their need by putting on a power display of His own. He did extra-miraculous miracles, demonstrating to the people that He was more powerful than any of their religious substitutes that kept them in spiritual darkness. He knew what they really needed was Himself! By offering Himself through the gospel, our God rescued them out of their spiritual darkness and brought them into His wonderful light.

LIFE IN THE DARKNESS

Everyone has experienced total darkness in their lives at some time. That might include being in a dark room at night, inside a cave when the lights are turned off for dramatic effect, or walking down a dark street.

Think of a time when you were in a physically dark place. How did that make you feel?

What did you do to get out of that dark place?

The Bible says that every human is born into the kingdom of spiritual darkness. And we have an enemy who does whatever he can to keep people in that darkness.

Read 2 Corinthians 4:4.

What does our spiritual enemy do?

Why?

Men and women who don't know Christ have blinded minds. They cannot see the light. They live in darkness. In Ephesians 2, Paul described life in this blinded dark condition and the forces working to influence those living in the darkness.

Read Ephesians 2:1-3.

Before knowing Christ, what is true about any person (verse 1)?

What do they follow (verse 2)?

Before trusting in Christ, you were not only blind and living in darkness. You were also spiritually dead. And a lot of substitute powers are influencing spiritually blind and dead people.

You learned in Lesson One that the ruler of the kingdom of the air is Satan, also known in the Bible as the devil. It is Satan and the evil spirits called demons who are part of the "rule and authority, power and dominion" under Jesus' feet in Ephesians 1:20-22. Yet, they are at work in those "who are disobedient" in the world. The world and the devil are substitute powers fighting God to gain control over humans.

> *Besides following the ways of the devil and the world, what other choices do unbelievers make (verse 3)?*

The sinful nature is also called "the flesh" in the Bible. It is that part of the human personality that is in rebellion against God. Living by the flesh is a substitute for living according to God's power and ways. We'll talk more about this in Lesson 6. For now, let's learn more about the life of the unbeliever.

Read Ephesians 4:17-19.

Paul's use of "the Gentiles" in this passage is a reference to those who are still unbelievers. It's not referring to the Gentile Christians. But many of the Ephesians who had been Gentiles remembered what life was like for them.

> *How are the unbelievers described in verse 18 (first half)?*

> *Why are they in that condition (verse 18, second half)?*

> *What behavior results (verse 19)?*

Following the desires and thoughts of the sinful nature leads to skewed thinking and darkened understanding. There's that blindness again. Hardening of hearts feeds their ignorance about God. Losing all sensitivity leads to giving oneself over to gratifying every kind of fleshly desire just like we read in Ephesians 2:3. And unbelievers are separated from the life of God. They are blind and dead because substitute powers are not life-giving.

Read Ephesians 2:12.

What is true about unbelievers?

The condition of the unbeliever is hopeless and helpless.

Do you remember what it was like when you were in spiritual darkness like that? Do you know someone still in darkness like that?

THE RESCUE FROM DARKNESS

But God had compassion on all of us who were living in darkness. He is the light to lead us out of it.

Read John 1:5.

What is true about God's light?

God's light is shining in the darkness. And no matter how bad your situation is, the darkness of this world, the devil, or your own sinful flesh cannot overcome God's light that leads you to being rescued. He rescues you and brings you into His light.

Read Ephesians 2:4-7.

What motivated God to act on our behalf (verse 4)?

What did He do for us (verse 5)?

Through whom is God's kindness expressed to us (verse 7)?

Read Ephesians 2:8-9.

Three important words are found in these two verses. Let's make sure we understand what they mean.

➢ GRACE: Unmerited favor, an undeserved gift

➢ SAVED: Rescued, spared from God's anger against sin

➢ FAITH: Belief, trust, commitment of mind and heart

How are you saved (verse 8)?

How are you not saved and why (verse 9)?

From what are you saved or rescued? Consider what you learned in Ephesians 2:1-3.

Grace provided your salvation and relationship with God. You didn't deserve it nor did you earn it by any good works. Rather, it is a free gift from God that you accepted when you received Christ through faith.

You are rescued from the kingdom of darkness in which you were born. You are rescued from your former way of life and the evil influences on you. You are rescued from being spiritually dead resulting in eternal separation from God. You are rescued from God's anger against sin. All of that is part of your salvation.

You are rescued through your faith. Simply put, faith is a full commitment to Christ. Instead of believing in your own ability to earn God's favor, you now trust in what Christ has done for you. That's biblical faith.

Read Ephesians 2:10.

Once you are saved, you are a new creation in Christ (God's handiwork). What new purpose does He have for you?

As part of your new creation with a new purpose, God has some good works for you to do. These good works are not for you to gain your salvation or even keep it. They are ways for you to express your love and gratitude for what God has already done for you. It's a win/win!

YOUR TREASURE IN CHRIST

God calls people out of darkness into His wonderful light. When we were helpless, His love, mercy, grace, kindness, and life-giving spirit stepped in to meet our need. His power rescues anyone who comes to Him through faith in His Son Jesus Christ. That's all it takes to be rescued.

Jesus Christ came to rescue you from that condition. This letter to the Ephesians was written by the Holy Spirit through Paul to show them and you how to overcome whatever is coming against you. There may be evil spiritual forces behind the people, the habits, and the situations that are messing up your life. But the answer is not to try out everything available to see if something "sticks." The answer is found in what Jesus already provides to you in Himself.

You might be thinking to yourself, "Can a person who trusted in Christ know with certainty that she will spend eternity with God?" Great question!

Here's the great answer: You **can know** that you have a secure salvation. You **can be confident** in God's grace toward you that makes you alive in Christ. This spiritual life is forever.

> *Suppose you were standing before God and He asked you, "Why should I let you into my heaven?" What would you now say?*

You can answer, "I know I am saved by your grace through my faith in your Son Jesus Christ." You are in!

As soon as you trust in Christ to be your Savior, you begin a loving relationship with Him. You receive treasure that is yours to know and experience for the rest of your earthly life and beyond. When you trust in Christ, He is in your life forever. You will never be without Him. Your rescue from darkness is one of many treasures you have in Him.

The treasure you have in Jesus Christ is more powerful and valuable than anything you could substitute for Him.

REMEMBER THE TREASURE OF YOUR RESCUE FROM DARKNESS

Recommended: Listen to the podcast "REMEMBER THE TREASURE OF YOUR RESCUE FROM DARKNESS." Use the section below as a listener guide.

The Bible says that every human is born into the kingdom of darkness. And we have a spiritual enemy who keeps people in that darkness by blinding their minds so that they cannot see the light of the gospel (2 Corinthians 4:4). They live in darkness.

As you learned in Ephesians 2:1-3, people who don't know Christ are not only blind but are also spiritually dead. And a lot of substitute powers are influencing spiritually blind and dead people.

The substitute power of the world

Unbelievers follow the **ways of this world**. Men and women all over the internet claim to have their own solutions to the world's problems. You can follow all kinds of seemingly good advice for living your life. Yet, most of those substitute ways for approaching life do not lead to God's way of approaching life. The ways of the world are a substitute power for living.

The substitute power of the devil

The Bible says that there is a **spirit** now at work in those who are disobedient (Ephesians 2:2). That spirit is Satan, also known as "the devil." He is in rebellion against God and so are those evil spirits with him called "demons." Satan and the demons are angels created by God at the beginning of creation. But they chose to rebel against God instead.

Satan and his demonic forces do everything they can to thwart the good purposes of God. They gain control over people through deception, counterfeits, fear, manipulation, torment, and rebellion against authority. Demons are behind any personality or teaching that entices you to rely on them more than on Christ. These demonic forces offer a substitute power for living. But their way always encourages disobedience against God.

The substitute power of the flesh

Another power at work in humans is the flesh, also called the "sinful nature" in the Bible (Ephesians 2:3). It is that part of the human spirit that is in rebellion against God. The result is pretty ugly. Following the desires and thoughts of the sinful nature leads to skewed thinking, hardened hearts, losing sensitivity to what is good, and eventually gratifying oneself with every kind of fleshly desire (Ephesians 4:17-19). This living by the power of the flesh is a substitute power for living.

The world, the devil, and the flesh are very powerful substitutes. But spiritually dead people are not necessarily criminals or immoral people. Someone who is controlled by the devil, the world, and the flesh could be a good person who receives applause from the world for doing good works. One writer described such a person as being moral, proud, and individual. She thinks she is self-governed and has no need of God.

There are a lot of blind people walking around. And in their blindness-darkness-deadness, they are groping along the walls to find their way to a door that will give them purpose in life. Most don't even know they're blind until they see a light illuminating the way to something more beautiful than what they've ever known.

God acted to rescue us from that wretched condition.

God was motivated by His great love for us and His mercy for our wretched condition. Because of that love, He sent His Son to die on the cross to rescue us.

Three words associated with God are more powerful than any of those 3 influences holding you in darkness (the world, the devil, and the flesh). We find those beautiful words in Ephesians 2:8-9.

> *"For it is by **grace** you have been **saved**, through **faith**—and this is not from yourselves, it is the gift of God—not by works, so that no one can boast."*

Those three powerful words are grace, saved, and faith. Let's look at them more closely.

Grace

Grace is undeserved favor. It is a gift we don't deserve. Because of Christ's finished work on the cross, God extends an invitation to every human living in darkness. The invitation is this: come out of the darkness. Be rescued. No one on planet Earth deserves this gift of rescue. God offers this to us because of His great love for us. By His grace, you have been rescued from the darkness.

Saved

The rescue is our salvation. God saves us from the darkness of sin and also from His own judgment against sin. That's what salvation means. We are rescued by our faith in Jesus Christ. And we are made alive so we are no longer dead. That happens the moment you place your faith in Jesus Christ.

Faith

What is faith? Faith is not a blind belief or mindless gullibility. It is not a life of passivity and doing nothing. Faith is also not a religious feeling like a tingle or good feeling from performing some ritual.

So if faith is not that, what is it? The word "faith" means a "belief, trust, and commitment of mind and heart to something or someone."

> ➢ Faith is **intelligent**. That means first you need to know about that something or someone. It is based on information about the object of your faith.

> ➢ Faith is also **decisive**. It involves the element of assent or agreement that the information about that someone or something is true.

> ➢ Faith **requires an act of the will**. Any conscious choice that involves trust, reliance, or dependence on someone or something requires a deliberate action to choose to trust the information.

Simply put, faith is placing your trust in God and His Word. It is a full commitment to Christ. When you received Christ, you put your trust in Christ and His death for your sin. Instead of believing in your own ability to earn God's favor, you now trust that you have been reconciled to God through what Christ has done for you.

By God's grace, you are saved through your faith. It is by your faith in Christ alone that you are rescued from your blindness, darkness, and deadness.

God rescues you from the destruction caused by sin. He offers you this salvation by His grace that is given to you. It is the gift of God—not by works, so that no one can boast of their efforts. Your response to God's gift of rescue is to say, "Yes. I accept." That's a response of faith. You can know that you are saved by God's grace through your faith in Son Jesus Christ." No doubts about it!

Faith is fed by knowing God.

Trust or faith is always an issue of credibility. It is hard to trust God if you don't know Him. Faith is fed by knowing God. The more you know Him, the easier it is to trust Him. You don't have more faith by talking about faith. Getting to know the object of your faith, your God, increases your confidence in Him. The Bible describes that confidence as having your feet firmly planted on solid rock with God as your Rock. He is a trustworthy God.

> God wants you to follow His Son. But you won't follow someone you don't trust. You can't trust someone you don't know, and you cannot know Christ apart from His Word. (Rebecca Carrell, heartstrongfaith.com)

That's why it is so important to study the Bible. We have not physically seen the risen Christ as the apostles did. We must see Him through eyes of faith and allow the gospels to leap off the page revealing our Lord.

God's power rescues you through your faith in Jesus Christ.

God rescues people out of spiritual darkness, and He brings them into His wonderful light. When you were helpless, His love, mercy, grace, kindness, and life-giving spirit stepped in to meet your need. His power rescues anyone who comes to Him through faith in His Son Jesus Christ. That's all it takes to be rescued.

No one doing this study is from a rougher background than those Ephesians. Did you grow up being deceived? Were you mistreated? Do you still struggle with relying on your own power to make your way in the world?

Jesus Christ came to rescue you from that condition. Have you made that choice by faith in Jesus Christ? If you aren't sure, I invite you to do so today, right now.

Please consider praying this prayer along with me:

> Thank you, God, for loving me and for sending Your Son Jesus to die for my sins. I trust in Jesus Christ to be my personal Savior and turn my entire life over to You. Thank you for rescuing me. Amen.

If you did that, tell someone.

As soon as you trust in Christ to be your Savior, you begin a loving relationship with Him. You receive treasure that is yours to know and experience for the rest of your earthly life and beyond. When you trust in Christ, He is in your life forever. You will never be without Him. Ever!

Let Jesus satisfy your heart with the confidence that the treasure you have in Him is more powerful and valuable than anything you could substitute for Him]

> *If you are wondering about the destiny of babies and small children who die, see my blog "Be Confident That Your Baby Is in Heaven" at melanienewton.com.*

Reflect

> **Consider what your life in spiritual darkness was like. How has your life changed since God rescued you from that darkness and brought you into His wonderful light? Thank Him for what He has done.**

> *Pray: Thank God for the treasure He has given you in Jesus Christ. Ask Him to help you recognize anything that you are substituting for Him. Ask Him to help you trust in Him alone for the power to be "successful" in life.*

The Treasure of Every Spiritual Blessing in Christ

"Praise be to the God and Father of our Lord Jesus Christ, who has blessed us in the heavenly realms with every spiritual blessing in Christ." (Ephesians 1:3, NIV)

Pray: Lord Jesus, please teach me through this lesson.

God calls people out of darkness into His wonderful light. When we were helpless, His love, mercy, grace, kindness, and life-giving spirit stepped in to meet our need. His power rescues anyone who comes to Him through faith in His Son Jesus Christ.

When you trust in Christ, you are rescued from the kingdom of darkness in which you were born. You are rescued from your former way of life and the evil influences on you. You are rescued from being spiritually dead resulting in eternal separation from God. You are rescued from God's anger against sin. All of that is part of your salvation. But there's more!

From the moment you say yes to Jesus and the relationship He offers you, you are brought to a place of blessing where you are accepted, loved, and lavished with spiritual riches—greater riches than you could ever imagine belonging to you. In Ephesians 1:3-14, Paul lists spiritual riches that have belonged to you from the moment you placed your faith in Christ.

YOUR BLESSING JEWELS

Read Ephesians 1:3-14.

> "It is as though (Paul) was ecstatically opening a treasure chest, lifting its jewels with his hands, letting them cascade through his fingers, and marveling briefly at them as they caught his eye." (*Dr. Constable's Notes on Ephesians 2020 Edition*, p. 15)

Looking just at verse 3, with what has God blessed us?

"To bless" is to bestow favor upon someone or something. A blessing is the favor or benefit being bestowed. The one who receives this blessing in verse 3 is the one who is "in Christ."

These blessings are associated with something called "the heavenly realms." Paul used this phrase 5 times in Ephesians. The heavenly realms are the unseen world of spiritual reality. God and all angelic beings, both good and bad, operate in this unseen dimension. We learned about all those forces in the last 2 lessons. Any time you ask God to heal someone or work in someone's life, you are thinking about this unseen world of "the heavenly realms."

Are you "in Christ?" Are you then the recipient of every spiritual blessing?

How does that make you feel?

Because of His love for us, God chooses to lavish upon us every spiritual blessing He has to give. These are the jewels in our God-given treasure chest. Let's look at these blessing jewels as though they are individual gemstones.

Read Ephesians 1:4 again.

For those who are in Christ, God has chosen for them to be what?

To be "holy" means to be "set apart from sin." That is how God views you now. By faith in Jesus Christ, God declares you blameless in His sight. When He looks on you, He sees you as perfected because you are in His Son, covered by Christ's perfection. You are no longer flawed by sin.

How long ago did God make that decision about believers in Christ?

To be chosen means that God had a plan from the beginning for all believers to be **in Christ** and to be made holy and blameless in Him. God put Christ and us together in His mind from the beginning. That was His plan.

Paul's reference to Christians being chosen is significant. Up to this point, the Jews were considered God's chosen people. You will readily see that as you study the Old Testament. Now, we know God had another chosen people who were actually chosen first—before the creation of the world, before the Jews were selected.

Read Ephesians 1:5 again.

The term "predestined" means determined or decided beforehand. God had pre-determined something.

God predetermined what for you?

Why did He do this?

What does it mean to be adopted?

Adoption to "sonship" is a legal term meaning the adopted child is granted all the privileges of a natural child, including inheritance rights. It has nothing to do with gender. It has everything to do with status.

Jesus' crucifixion was part of God's predetermined plan. Believers being conformed to the likeness of Jesus is part of God's predetermined plan. Here in verse 5, God predetermined our adoption as His children (sons & daughters).

Read Ephesians 1:6-8 again.

According to verse 7, what do you have?

Redemption is a term related to our rescue from the kingdom of darkness as we learned about in the last lesson. Christ paid your price for redemption with His own blood. You then become the possession of a loving, merciful God and can live in the security of your freedom from bondage to sin.

Forgiveness is rescue from your debt of sin. God transferred your sin to a substitute, Jesus, and it was taken away. According to Colossians 2:13-14, all of your sin—past, present, and future—was nailed to the cross. Your forgiveness is complete and continual.

What else has God lavished upon you (verses 7-8)?

What does the word "lavish" mean?

From verse 6, what else do you learn about God's lavishing His grace to you?

God's grace is extravagantly reckless toward us. Grace is what God does to make men and women acceptable to Him. We don't deserve such favor. And we can never earn such favor.

Grace is summed up in the name, person, and work of the Lord Jesus Christ. We receive this favor or acceptance from God as a free gift through faith in Christ. And grace is continually being given to us for daily living as well.

Knowing you have been redeemed, forgiven, and lavished with God's grace, how does that make you feel toward God?

Read Ephesians 1:9-10 again.

A mystery in the Bible is something that is kept hidden in the heart of God until He chooses to reveal it. God has made known to believers the mystery of His will purposed (determined) in Christ.

Later in Ephesians, Paul wrote that part of the mystery being revealed is that the Gentiles and the Jews are joined together through the gospel into one body called the Body of Christ. We'll discover more about this in the Lesson 5.

What is God's future plan (verse 10, second half)?

When will He put that into effect (verse 10, first half)?

What God planned in the past and enabled in the present through Christ and the cross will be put into effect universally in the future. We get to know about this now. We know the what, but we don't know the when.

Read Ephesians 1:13-14 again.

A seal in New Testament times was a form of identification used to authenticate and protect legal documents. A document was rolled up, a small pool of melted wax was placed across the overlapping edges, and a signet ring belonging to the official was pressed into the wax. The seal carried with it the idea of ownership, identification, security, permanence, and completeness.

> *With whom are you sealed?*

> *What does that seal guarantee for you?*

Our God is one God but three persons—God the Father, God the Son (Jesus), and God the Holy Spirit. The Holy Spirit is the first gift we receive from God when we trust in Jesus for salvation. He is the one who gives spiritual life to the spiritually blind and dead person the moment she believes in Jesus. He delivers to us all the blessing jewels in our treasure chest. He also marks every Christian with the seal of God's ownership.

The treasure you have in Jesus Christ is more powerful and valuable than anything you could substitute for Him.

YOUR TREASURE IN CHRIST

> *How do you feel about what God has done and will do for you?*

> *Why are these treasures you have been given in Jesus Christ more valuable than anything you could provide for yourself or what the world could give you?*

SEEK THE TREASURE

REJOICE IN THE TREASURE OF EVERY SPIRITUAL BLESSING IN CHRIST

Recommended: Listen to the podcast *"REJOICE IN THE TREASURE OF EVERY SPIRITUAL BLESSING IN CHRIST."* Use the section below as a listener guide.

You receive every spiritual blessing in Christ (Ephesians 1:3) because of Christ's finished work on the cross and His resurrection. These blessings are associated with "the heavenly realms"—the unseen world of spiritual reality where God and all angelic beings, both good and bad, work.

After Christ was raised from the dead, He ascended into heaven and was exalted over all the powers in that unseen world—angels, demons, and Satan (Ephesians 1:20-22). In God's mind, all believers are in Christ there (Ephesians 2:6). Because of His love for us, God chooses to lavish upon us spiritual blessing jewels that fill our God-given treasure chest.

The blessing jewel of chosen to be holy and blameless (Ephesians 1:4)

What "chose us" can mean: Just from Ephesians 1:4, we know the word "chosen" can mean that God had a plan from the beginning for all believers to be **in Christ** and to be made holy and blameless in Him. God put Christ and us together in His mind from the beginning. As soon as someone believes in Christ, the Bible says they are considered "chosen" and "elect" from that moment forward.

Before Christ came, the Jews were the ones considered God's chosen people. Now, we know God had another chosen people who were actually chosen first—before the creation of the world, before the Jews were selected. God's plan created a new people for Himself through Christ. Whether Jew or Gentile, all Christians are now called chosen.

What "chose us" cannot mean: To be chosen does not mean that God chose some to love and some to not love before any were ever born. God loves everyone, and everyone can believe in Him (John 3:16). And it doesn't mean that some people shouldn't be told about the gospel because God hasn't chosen them to be saved. The Bible teaches that God wants all people to believe in Him and be saved.

If you have accepted Jesus Christ as Savior and trust in Him alone for salvation, you are saved and you are, therefore, **chosen** because your identity is in Christ, not in yourself.

To be holy and blameless in Christ: Believers are chosen by God for a purpose—to be made holy and blameless in Christ. By faith in Jesus Christ, God declares you holy in His sight. To be "holy" means to be declared "set apart from sin." That gives you a different status before God. Every believer has been set apart as God's special, beloved possession for His exclusive use. God declares you holy because of your faith in Jesus Christ, not your behavior. You are also "being made holy" in your thoughts, words, and actions by the ongoing work of the Holy Spirit. In God's eyes, you are perfected and no longer flawed. Blameless.

The blessing jewel of predestined for adoption (Ephesians 1:5)

What "predestined" does mean: Predestined does mean that God had determined something beforehand. Jesus' crucifixion, believers being conformed to the likeness of Jesus, and believers being adopted by God as His sons & daughters are all part of God's predetermined plan. You as His adopted child receive the full inheritance that God gave to Jesus to give to you. It has nothing to do with gender. It has everything to do with status. You are a daughter of Almighty God. God predestined you for that.

What "predestined" cannot mean: Predestined does not mean that you are a puppet with no control over your "destiny." Individuals believe in Christ and receive all the spiritual blessings plus heaven. Or individuals choose to not believe and receive nothing plus eternal separation from God.

The blessing jewels of redemption, forgiveness, and being lavished with God's grace (Ephesians 1:6-8)

Redemption: Everyone born on this planet is born into slavery to sin where the slave master "sin" calls the shots, and they obey too easily. But you are released from all of that when you trust in Jesus Christ. The Bible calls this "redemption."

God redeems you to rescue you from the dominion of darkness and bring you into His wonderful light. Christ paid your price for redemption with His own blood. You have been released and are no longer in bondage to sin and guilt. You have become the possession of a loving, merciful God and can live in the security of your freedom from bondage to sin. You have a new master now with greater power living inside of you—the Spirit of God Himself. He enables you to live in a way that pleases God.

Forgiveness of sins: Our debt of sin before God is so enormous we could never pay for it all. We carry the guilt of our sins like a heavy burden, weighing us down. But God stepped in and did for us what we couldn't do for ourselves. He transferred our sin to a substitute, Jesus, and it was taken away.

Once you place your faith in Jesus Christ, whatever you've done that was wrong in God's eyes from the time you were born through the time of your death has been canceled and taken away (Colossians 2:13-14). All of it was nailed to the cross—past, present and future. Forgiveness is complete and continual. In Christ, you possess forgiveness of sins (Ephesians 1:7). You have been forgiven and are no longer burdened by your sin and guilt.

Being lavished with His grace: To lavish means "to bestow something in generous or extravagant quantities." God's grace is poured out upon us richly. God is not stingy with His grace. God's grace is extravagantly reckless toward us.

Grace is what God does to make men and women acceptable to Him. We don't deserve such favor. And we can never earn such favor. Grace is summed up in the name, person, and work of the Lord Jesus Christ. We receive this favor or acceptance from God as a free gift through faith in Christ. And grace is given to us for daily living as well.

The blessing jewel of revelation (Ephesians 1:9-10)

A mystery in the Bible is something that is kept hidden in the heart of God until He chooses to reveal it. One mystery God has revealed to us is His future plan to bring all things in heaven and on earth together under the powerful authority of Christ (Ephesians 1:9-10). We are part of Jesus' heavenly Kingdom now. One day, we will be part of His Kingdom on earth. We know the "what," but we don't know the "when."

The blessing jewel of being sealed and secured (Ephesians 1:13)

Remember that the Holy Spirit is God just as much as the Father is God and Jesus Christ is God. At the moment we trust in Christ, the Spirit gives us spiritual life, delivers to us all the blessing jewels in our treasure chest, and marks us with the seal of God's ownership. This "sealing" means that...

- ➢ You are wanted, valuable, and important.

- ➢ You are God's child and will receive all the inheritance promised to His children—such as heaven, new bodies, and living with Christ in His kingdom.

- ➢ You are prepared through all your blessing jewels for your life in Christ on earth and also for life in heaven.

God the Father does the sealing. The Holy Spirit is the seal. It takes place the moment you believe in Jesus Christ. Nowhere are you exhorted to ask for it so it must be universal and immediate. It is also permanent. There is no power greater than God who can break the seal, including you.

The Holy Spirit present in us is our security that we are God's possession, that He won't forget about us when Jesus returns, that we go to be with Him when we die, that our sins will never again count against us, that we are new creatures, and that all those spiritual blessing jewels in Christ are ours forever.

These are your spiritual blessings **in Christ** to be enjoyed now, meeting the deepest needs of your heart. These have nothing to do with your finances, your health, or your earthly family status. They will never rust, rot, or disappear. These treasures given to you in Christ are more valuable than anything you could provide for yourself.

Let Jesus satisfy your heart with the confidence that the treasure you have in Him is more powerful and valuable than anything you could substitute for Him.

Reflect

Thank God now for those spiritual blessing jewels you have received from Him. Go ahead. Let your heart overflow in praise and thanksgiving for the treasure you have in Christ. Use prayer, prose, poetry, drawing, song, or whatever you choose.

The Treasure of Being Dearly Loved

"I pray that you, being rooted and established in love, may have power ... to grasp how wide and long and high and deep is the love of Christ, and to know this love that surpasses knowledge..." (Ephesians 3:17b-19a, NIV)

Pray: Lord Jesus, please teach me through this lesson.

One of the top internet search phrases leading people to the website Bible.org is this question, "What does God think about me?" That could be a natural question for anyone to ask who does not already know the Bible's teachings. But a lot of times, that question reveals great insecurity, even among Christians. Perhaps this question is constantly rolling over in your mind. "What does God think about me?"

If you look at stuff on the internet and read through some devotionals and Bible studies, you'll run across teaching that focuses constantly on our sinfulness. And yes, every human is prone to sinfulness. But the good news of God's grace toward us and His life in us is often left out

No wonder many women look at their lives, which may be very messy compared to others, and think to themselves, "God must not like me as much as He does her." And "What must I do to make Him love me more?" Have you ever thought that way?

Stop it! Remember your treasure chest in Christ filled with beautiful things that God has given to you as His adopted daughter. In the last lesson, we fingered some of those jewels that you are given: chosen to be holy and blameless, forgiven of all sin, lavished with grace, and sealed by the Holy Spirit guaranteeing your inheritance—now and later.

And here's another blessing jewel for you. It truly answers that question, "What does God think about me?"

A FATHER'S LOVE

Read Ephesians 5:1-2.

What did Paul call the believers in verse 1?

To follow God's example means to do what (beginning of verse 2)?

How did Christ demonstrate His love for us (verse 2)?

Now you know the answer to that question, "What does God think about me?" As a Christian, you are a *dearly loved child* of God. You are dearly loved by God the Father and are dearly loved by our Savior Jesus Christ.

And our God who loves you dearly and has given you all those blessing jewels also wants a relationship with you. So He's given humans another gift that no other creature has—the gift of conversation. You and I have this gift to use in our relationship with Him. Using our words in conversation with God is called prayer. Prayer is not an "it." It's not a "to do." *It is an experience to enjoy.* Prayer is a conversation with Someone who loves you dearly.

Read Ephesians 3:12.

Because we are in Christ, what may we do?

To approach means to move toward, to have access, to come near. We, as believers, may enter the presence of the living God.

Why may we do that with freedom and confidence? Hint: remember our blessing jewels from Lesson 3.

Think of a close relationship you enjoy with someone now. How did that relationship develop? What did you intentionally do to get to know one another? What risks did you take?

God wants us to know Him this way too. We are each in a unique relationship with God. It can't be measured by minutes or as a "to do" list to check off. It takes intentional time and risk.

Maybe something in your past makes you uncomfortable about praying. God wants you to get over whatever that is. He wants you to talk to Him. He wants you to enjoy a relationship with Someone who loves you dearly. And He gives you the gift of knowing Him so that you feel a close relationship with Him. That's another spiritual blessing jewel.

THE GIFT OF KNOWING HIM

Read Ephesians 1:15-17.

Paul asked God to give the Ephesian Christians what (verse 17, first half)?

So that they may do what (verse 17 second half)?

The one who lavished you with adoption, forgiveness, and grace is the giver of all good gifts. So Paul prayed for the giver of all good gifts to give believers something that God promises—wisdom and revelation to know Him better.

That word "know" means "going beyond objective facts to **knowing God intimately** as in "closely acquainted and familiar." We can know Him personally, as a close friend. What a gift!

"Wisdom" means insight into the true nature of things. Revelation is unveiling a mystery, which we talked about in the last lesson. In this case, the mystery is God Himself.

We need wisdom because there's a lot of junk out there about God. That's why it's so important to really get to know the God of the Bible. We can never know all there is to know about God. There'll always be some mystery about Him. But there's plenty enough revealed in the Bible that we can know Him truthfully.

> How often we miss the conscious presence of God with the result that we only know God by hearsay! ... Anyone can write a book now that will sell—just give it a title like, *Seventeen Ways to Get Things from God!* You will have immediate sales. ... Many people seem to be interested in knowing God for what they can get out of Him. ... God wants to give Himself. He wants to impart Himself with His gifts. Any gift that He would give us would be incomplete if it were separated from the knowledge of God Himself. (A.W. Tozer, *Tozer Speaks: Volume 1*)

That's what God wants for you. You can know God intimately. Just ask for it.

You can also know the good God has for you.

KNOWING GOD'S GIFTS

Read Ephesians 1:18-19.

Wisdom and revelation will open up the eyes of your heart (your mind and inner spirit) to be enlightened (flooded with light so you can see well) so you may know some things very important to know. Paul's use of the word "know" here means "to know facts with certainty."

What good things can we know with certainty (verse 18)?

What other good thing can we know with certainty (verse 19, first half)?

His hope and riches for you (verse 18) refer back to all those blessing jewels that we covered in Ephesians 1:3-14 (Lesson 3). Those belong to you now and throughout eternity.

His incomparably great power for you as a believer (verse 19) is another blessing jewel. It's beyond comparison with anything else because it is so far above anything else available!

To the Ephesians, spiritual power was an impersonal force like electricity that one could harness and use to one's own advantage. You could manipulate the power. Magical formulas led to guaranteed results.

> *How have you been influenced to think of spiritual power (even God's power) as something to harness and use to your own advantage? To get what you want?*

The biblical view of spiritual power is this: Our personal **God uses His power to accomplish His own will and purposes.** He extends it to those who trust in Him to accomplish His will and purposes in their lives, also.

God's power for us is used to take care of us and to change us from the inside out as we trust Him. God's spiritual power is greater than anything we can try on our own, is available to every believer, and it rests in the person of God alone. That is true about prayer, also. The power in prayer is not in the act of praying. Otherwise, it's dependent on you doing it right. No, the power is always in the One to whom you are praying. The power is **in our prayer-listening God.**

In Ephesians chapter 3, Paul continued his previous thought about God's power in us and prayed for one more thing—the one thing that makes a relationship soar. That one thing is something for you to know with absolute certainty.

KNOWING GOD'S LOVE

Read Ephesians 3:16-19.

> *Out of God's riches for us, we can pray for Him to do what (verse 16)?*

So that what happens (verse 17, first half)?

Now, Jesus Christ already lives in the heart of every believer through the Holy Spirit. That word "dwell" means that Jesus is so at home in your heart that He is the dominating factor in your attitudes and behavior. That will be evident as you live each day. That's being strengthened by Christ's power in you as He overcomes your natural self-centered tendencies.

Being strengthened in Christ's power will help you to be what (verse 17, second half)?

To be rooted and established in love means to be grounded in it, stabilized by it. Why would this require Christ's power in your inner being?

What does Christ's power within us help us to grasp and know (verses 18-19)?

What confidence do you get from knowing the truth about how much God loves you?

"There is nothing you can do to do make God love you more!
There is nothing you can do to make God love you less! His love
is Unconditional, Impartial, Everlasting, Infinite, Perfect!"
(Richard Halverson, former chaplain U.S. Senate)

Wow! You are loved like that! God is not stingy with His love. The moment you believe in Jesus Christ, He **loves you dearly** just like that. The treasure you have in our Father God who loves you dearly is more powerful and valuable than anything or anyone you could substitute for Him.

Let's look at what bubbled up out of Paul's heart as he dwelled on God's amazing love for him. Let it bubble up out of yours, also.

Read Ephesians 3:20-21.

Write verse 20 in the space below.

As your Father God loves you dearly, where do you need Him to work in a way that is immeasurably more than you can ask or imagine? What will you trust Him for today?

YOUR TREASURE IN CHRIST

Do you struggle with believing that God loves you? Why?

The Bible says that you are "**dearly loved**." Write this phrase on your mirror or someplace where you will see it often. **"I am dearly loved by my Father God."** And put Ephesians 5:1 below that. The next time you ponder what God says or thinks about you, remember this truth.

SEEK THE TREASURE

BASK IN THE TREASURE OF BEING DEARLY LOVED

Recommended: *Listen to the podcast "BASK IN THE TREASURE OF BEING DEARLY LOVED." Use the section below as a listener guide.*

In our lesson today, we discovered another blessing jewel that should make your heart soar. According to Ephesians 5:1, you are a dearly loved child of God. Dearly loved. Grasp that truth. And here is the great news. Our God who loves you dearly and has given you all those other blessing jewels wants a relationship with you. So He's given humans another gift that no other creature has—the gift of conversation. And through this gift, you can enjoy a relationship with this wonderful God who loves you dearly.

Studies say that women have about 20,000 words to use up each day. The God of the Universe wants to hear some of those from us—whether thinking them or speaking them. Isn't that amazing?

Prayer is conversation with someone who loves you dearly.

Using our words in conversation with God is called prayer. This could happen during a structured time of prayer each day. Or it could be as you do your daily tasks and interact with people. God wants you to bare your soul, to ask Him for what you need and what others need, to thank Him and praise Him. He wants you to remember that He is present with you and simply converse with Him just like you think about and talk to people you love all day long.

Every time the subject of prayer comes up, the tendency is to start feeling guilty for not doing it right or getting busy and forgetting all about praying. Thankfully, prayer is not an "it" or a "to do." It is an experience to enjoy. Prayer is a conversation with Someone who loves you dearly.

> *"In Him (that's Jesus) and through faith in Him we may approach God with freedom and confidence." (Ephesians 3:12)*

You can approach the God of the universe with freedom and confidence because of what Christ has done for you and your identity being in Him. Based on that, here are some truths we can know about prayer.

Prayer truth #1: God hears your prayer because of Jesus in you.

God hears your prayer because of Jesus in you, and you in Him. In God's eyes, you are seated in Christ, right next to God the Father (Ephesians 2:6).

You can picture yourself looking at God the Father and saying, "Father, I need a word of encouragement from you today." Or as you are seated in Christ saying, "Did you see that, Lord Jesus? What should I do now?"

What an incredible privilege to enjoy—resting in Christ and talking to Him about anything and everything that matters to your heart like you would do with your best friend on your phone.

Prayer truth #2: God doesn't require "special language."

God doesn't require "special" language like "thee" and "thou" to get His attention. Those words were commonly used in the King James Version written 400 years ago. They are not used in everyday language today. You have the freedom to use them or not use them.

Prayer truth #3: God assists you as you pray.

When you are too distressed or distracted to even know the right words to pray, the Holy Spirit who is living inside you says your words for you. He carries the right message to God the Father from your heart to His (Romans 8:26). And Jesus is doing the same as He acts on your behalf (Romans 8:34).

Prayer truth #4: You have direct access to God.

You can go to God directly with whatever is on your heart. No one who is dead or alive is any closer to God than you are. You are seated in Christ with God's Spirit inside of you. You don't need the help of someone with the title of "Saint" or any other title to get God to hear your prayer. So feel free to talk directly to God yourself.

Prayer truth #5: No formula guarantees results.

There's no formula for prayer that you can use to guarantee results. There are some tools out there to guide you in your structured prayer time. But there's no formula to conversation with Someone who loves you dearly. You don't use a formula to talk to your parents, or best friend, or spouse. You don't have to do that with God. The best prayer comes straight from the heart.

Neither do you have to say, "in Jesus' name," although that becomes a habit for us to use without thinking. "In Jesus' name" is not a magical phrase. The attitude of praying in Jesus' name is asking according to what Jesus would ask. It's a spirit of obedience and submission to His will more than your own. It's not a formula.

Prayer truth #6: Prayer flows from knowing God.

Prayer is conversation with Someone who not only loves you dearly but also gives you the gift of knowing Him intimately. The one who lavished us with adoption, forgiveness, and grace is the giver of all good gifts. One of these gifts is to know Him. That word "know" means going beyond objective facts to knowing God intimately as in "closely acquainted and familiar." We can know Him personally, as a close friend. What a gift! That's another spiritual blessing jewel and one that will certainly stimulate prayer in your life.

Knowing Him starts with studying the Scriptures to learn who this glorious Father God is who gives you an identity and purpose in His Son Jesus Christ. Then, the Holy Spirit uses that Scripture to teach you about God and gives you an intimate awareness of His presence.

We will never know all there is to know about God. There'll always be some mystery about Him. But there's plenty enough revealed in the Bible that we can know Him truthfully. Then, you can discern all the false information the world gives you and delete it from influencing you. God wants you to be able to recognize His hand in your life, His power at work for you in specific answers to prayer that could only be from God. You can know God intimately like that. Paul wrote, "Ask for it." So...ask for it.

Firmly grasp how much you are dearly loved.

As you get to know God, you will really be able to firmly grasp the immensity of how much you are loved! Jesus wants this to be deeply rooted in you. You can know this love intimately and experientially. It's not just head knowledge. As a believer in Christ, you are an individual recipient of God's personal love for you as His child.

Through God's power **in** you, you can grasp God's love **for** you (Ephesians 3:16-19). God enables you to overcome your insecurities and doubts and comparisons in order to know and experience His love. That's very important for you as a believer.

Have you heard that God loves you but your brain is telling you, "No way!" Or maybe you know in your head that God loves you, but you just don't feel it in your heart. It's okay to feel God's love for you. God wants you to really know it. You can ask for this. Romans 5:5 says that God pours His love into your heart. You can know the love of God for you. Grasp it! And allow yourself to feel it!

When you are confident in God's love for you, conversing with Him through prayer will be a natural response. God wants you to talk to Him. He wants you to enjoy a relationship with Someone who loves you dearly. And He gives you the gift of knowing Him so that you can feel a close relationship with Him.

It doesn't matter how many mistakes you've made in the past or what's in your bank account. Whether you've been a Christian for 3 weeks or 30 years, the Bible says you are dearly loved by your Father God—equally, no more, no less than every other Christian alive today or in the past.

Believer, you are dearly loved! You can bask in that treasure.

Let Jesus satisfy your heart with the confidence that the treasure you have in Him is more powerful and valuable than anything you could substitute for Him.

Reflect

Read and reflect on the song lyrics below. Then, thank God for His incomparable great love for you. Ask Him for His power in your life to grasp how much you are dearly loved by God in Christ.

I'm forgiven because You were forsaken, I'm accepted, You were condemned. I am alive and well, Your spirit is within me, Because You died and rose again.
Amazing love, How can it be? That You, my King would die for me? Amazing love, I know it's true. It's my joy to honor You, In all I do, I honor You. ("You Are My King," Chris Tomlin)

Pray: Thank God for the treasure He has given you in Jesus Christ. Ask Him to help you recognize anything that you are substituting for Him. Ask Him to help you trust in Him alone for the power to be "successful" in life.

The Treasure of the Church

5

"...we will grow to become... the mature body of him who is the head, that is, Christ. From him the whole body, joined and held together by every supporting ligament, grows and builds itself up in love, as each part does its work." (Ephesians 4:15-16, NIV)

Pray: Lord Jesus, please teach me through this lesson.

As a Christian, you are given the treasure of being a dearly loved child of God. And our God who loves you dearly and has given you all those blessing jewels also wants a relationship with you. So He's given you the gift of conversation to use in your relationship with Him through prayer.

God also wants you to know Him intimately and to experience His great love for you. For that, He has given you wisdom and revelation to know Him better as you would know a very close friend. And His Holy Spirit inside you strengthens your inner spirit to be able to grasp how much God loves you and is for you. All of these things you receive personally from God by your faith in His Son Jesus Christ. It is a privilege to enjoy personal fellowship with God.

But our God knows that while we are alive on this earth, you and I need to be with others who love Him. The way for us to enjoy fellowship with other believers is in God's awesome family on earth called the Church.

How did this awesome Church family begin? And for what purpose? We learn the answers to those questions and more from Paul's letter to the Ephesians.

A Little Bit of History

Before Christ, there were basically two groups of people in God's eyes— the Jews and the non-Jews. The Jews were in a covenant relationship with God based upon the Mosaic Law, which God had given to the ancient nation of Israel. The other group were those not born as Jews, often called Gentiles or Greeks in the Bible.

Read Ephesians 2:12.

How does the Bible describe the status of the non-Jews before they heard and accepted the gospel of Jesus Christ?

The non-Jews were separated because they did not know God by faith. They were excluded because they were not in the covenant relationship with God based on the Mosaic Law. And they were foreigners to the promises of God. As outsiders, they lived in a world without God and without hope because what they worshiped as gods (their idols) could give them nothing good.

Before Christ, a non-Jew could join the Jewish faith and start obeying the Mosaic Law. They didn't become Jews, but as "converts," they could participate in the Jewish religious ceremonies. That was the old plan. But our gracious and merciful God had a new plan with a different goal.

Read Ephesians 2:13-18.

What is now possible for those who were once far away from God and His promises (verse 13)?

What did Christ do to make this possible (verses 14-15, first half)?

What was His purpose (verses 15-16)?

What is now true for every believer in Christ (verse 18)?

God's plan had been kept a mystery before this time. In Lesson 3, you learned that a mystery in the Bible is something that is kept hidden in the heart of God until He chooses to reveal it. God chose to reveal one really big mystery to the believers in the first century AD.

Read Ephesians 3:4-6.

Because this mystery centers around what Christ would do, Paul called it the mystery of Christ.

According to verse 5, what do you learn about this mystery?

Was it only revealed to Paul? How do you know?

What is the mystery being revealed by God (verse 6)?

God's goal was to make both groups into one. Christ united what was once divided. This uniting included all people groups. No longer were there Jews and non-Jews. From then on, there are only Christians and those who reject Christ. And the new humanity created by God is the Body of Christ, also known as the Church (often written with a capital "C" to distinguish from local churches, i.e. "my church"). God's spirit power brought this new humanity into existence.

At the moment of salvation, the Spirit of God places every believer into the Body of Christ regardless of birth, ethnic background, age, or gender. All enter as equals and co-heirs of everything promised by God to all those who believe in Jesus Christ. All share equally in the spiritual blessing jewels. All are equally loved by God. All have equal access to God by one Spirit—the Holy Spirit indwelling them. This is the treasure of the Church.

THE CHURCH AS THE BODY OF CHRIST

The whole concept of the Church was very new to the people of Paul's day. So in Ephesians, Paul was guided by the Holy Spirit to use several images to illustrate what the Church is.

Read Ephesians 1:22-23.

What description did Paul use for the Church in verse 23?

Read Ephesians 2:19-22.

What words did Paul use to describe the Church in verse 19?

What image did Paul use to describe the Church in verses 20-22?

The Church is called the body of Christ. That's probably the one we know the best. The Church is also called God's people in His household. It is described as a building with Christ Jesus as the cornerstone of its foundation with all its parts joined together and rising to be a holy temple. And we are connected to this holy temple by the Spirit of God who lives inside each of us. Through God's Spirit, we all have equal access to God. That's the Church.

But even more important than those illustrations is one important truth.

Read Ephesians 4:15-16.

Who is the head of the Church (verse 15)?

From Him, what happens to the rest of the body (verse 16)?

The moment you became a Christian, the Holy Spirit placed you into this new family called the Church with Christ as its head. The Church is spread across the whole world and made up of every culture and language—all believers alive on planet earth now and those in heaven since the first century AD. It is not limited to a building, just as a natural family is not limited to their house. As Christ is the head of this universal family, all members are considered part of the Body of Christ.

THE TREASURE OF A LOCAL CHURCH FAMILY

While you are part of the universal Church, God wants you to be part of a local church family. It is like having relatives all over the world but living with your immediate family. A local church is a group of believers committed to worshiping Christ, teaching His Word, supporting each other as you follow Jesus together, and proclaiming the good news to others. You can enjoy relationships and spiritual growth within this Church community.

Why do you think it would be important for you to spend time with other Christians?

Read Ephesians 4:11-13.

Who has Christ provided to help you grow in your Christian life (verse 11)?

Remember that the apostles and prophets were those through whom God revealed His Word to people. This was especially important before the New Testament writings were gathered for all to read. Evangelists like Paul are still needed to communicate the gospel message for people to understand it and believe in Christ. Once anyone believes in Christ, pastors and teachers are needed in every local church.

What is the general responsibility of the pastors and teachers (verses 12-13)?

What is Christ's goal for every believer (verses 13 and 15)?

Read Ephesians 4:14.

What can happen if you are not being taught and built up in the faith to maturity?

Are there areas of life now where you feel tossed about by every wind of teaching?

Protection is one of the benefits of pastors and teachers doing their job to help you grow. Just as a house keeps people protected from harm, a good local church community can keep Christians safe from false teaching.

It is hard to recognize false teaching on your own. Being taught the truth within your local church keeps you from being deceived by the cunning and craftiness of those outside the church who want to rob you of the enjoyment of your spiritual blessing jewels and prevent you from bringing glory to God. Leaders that stay true to the Word of God will encourage the church community to stay true to God's Word, also.

Read Ephesians 4:15-16.

What is the benefit for the entire body of Christ when you grow in your faith (verse 16)?

Read Ephesians 4:12 again.

Notice the emphasis that the people in the local church are God's people.

Pastors and teachers are to equip God's people for what and why?

What could be considered "works of service" so that the body of Christ may be built up?

God has chosen to give something called spiritual gifts to individual believers in the local churches. Spiritual gifts are special abilities for ministry that are given by the Holy Spirit as He determines the need for the growth of Christ's church. The Spirit gives them to people at salvation or when needed within a local church. Some examples are teaching, shepherding (caring for a group), showing mercy to someone in need, and extending gracious hospitality.

"Works of service" could refer to Christians using their spiritual gifts to benefit their church community. Participating in your church community can help you to discover your spiritual gifts and learn how to use them to serve your church family well. You do this by serving people in love as opportunities present themselves to you.

"Works of service" also refers back to Ephesians 2:10.

Write that verse in the space below.

Just as fireplace logs burn more brightly when placed together, so Christians need each other for warmth and encouragement. The local church provides opportunity for you to enjoy this community. But enjoying community requires obedience to what our Head, Jesus Christ, desires for you.

Read John 13:34-35.

What is Jesus' command to His followers (verse 34)?

What effect can this have on those who do not know Jesus yet (verse 35)?

Enjoying community as part of a church family is called fellowship (from the Greek word meaning "sharing in common"). This sharing of our lives requires intentional and unconditional love for one another—the kind of love that God has for us. That's why Jesus' command said that relationships among believers should be marked by that kind of love for each other. This is not only mutually beneficial to Christians in a church family but is also one thing that definitely attracts those to Jesus who do not have a relationship with Him. There are others that we will see in the next lesson.

YOUR TREASURE IN CHRIST

In this lesson, you learned that you have a treasure in the Church as the Body of Christ. You received this treasure at the moment of salvation. And God has provided local church communities for you to enjoy loving relationships and continued spiritual growth.

Your local church community is a treasure for you as it:

> Helps you to grow strong in your faith and to know God better.

> Keeps you protected from being swayed by false teaching.

> Teaches you how to love others and model Christ's love to the world.

> Helps you to discover your spiritual gifts and learn how to use them to serve the church family.

> Acts as a source of encouragement to you.

The church is a treasure. And all the treasure you have in Christ, including membership in the Body of Christ, is more powerful and valuable than anything you could substitute for Him.

Praise and thank God for adopting you into His family and giving you a new community (the Body of Christ) in which to enjoy your life in Christ.

ENJOY YOUR TREASURE IN THE CHURCH

SEEK THE TREASURE

Recommended: Listen to the podcast "ENJOY YOUR TREASURE IN THE CHURCH." Use the section below as a listener guide.

Before Christ, there were basically two groups of people in God's eyes—the Jews and the non-Jews. A non-Jew could join the Jewish faith and start obeying the Mosaic Law. Some Jewish Christians, especially those who had been leaders in Jewish teaching, thought it still worked that way in the Church. But our gracious and merciful God had a new plan with a different goal.

He made the two groups (Jews and non-Jews) into one group by breaking down the one barrier that was the dividing wall, creating hostility between them. That one barrier was the Mosaic Law. Christ fulfilled every religious requirement of the Mosaic Law by His death on the cross. Both groups could now be reconciled through a common factor—the blood of Jesus Christ. The Law then became obsolete. All people groups would now be completely included in God's promises through the gospel of Jesus Christ.

From then on, there are only Christians and those who reject Christ. This new group of Christians is called the Church. Regardless of your birth, ethnic background, age, or gender, all members of the Church share equally in the promises of God and the spiritual blessing jewels. All are dearly loved by God and have equal access to God by His Holy Spirit indwelling them. This is the treasure of the Church.

What the Church is

The whole concept of the Church was so new to the people of Paul's day that he used several images to illustrate what the Church is.

> **The body of Christ with Christ as the Head (Ephesians 1:22-23; 4:15-16):** We can understand a body since we all have one. We understand how body parts are joined together, grow stronger through nourishment, and work to accomplish a purpose.

> **God's people in His household (Ephesians 2:19):** The Church is like a huge family spread across the whole world and made up of every culture and language—all believers alive on planet earth now and those in heaven since the first century AD. We can understand that image because we all have family of

some sort and ancestors who lived before us who were part of our family.

> **A building built upon Christ as the foundation (Ephesians 2:20-21):** The "cornerstone" was the crucial part of the foundation of a building. It was the stone the builder used to square every other stone, including the other foundation stones. This stone is Christ—the chief cornerstone. The rest of the foundation is laid by the apostles and prophets based on that one cornerstone. As this building rises up from the foundation, it is the new temple on earth where God's spirit dwells. God's temple dwelling is no longer in a physical building. The Spirit indwells every believer individually and collectively as a group. Our modern church buildings are not the house of God—only a place for the people of God to meet together.

The moment you became a Christian, the Holy Spirit placed you into this new family called the Church with Christ as its head. The Church is spread across the whole world and made up of every culture and language—all believers alive on planet earth now and those in heaven since the first century AD. It is not limited to a building, just as a natural family is not limited to their house. As Christ is the head of this universal family, all members are considered part of the Body of Christ. That includes every local church as well.

The treasure of a local church family

While you are part of the universal Church, God wants you to be part of a local church family. It is like having relatives all over the world but living with your immediate family. God has designed the local church to be an important aspect of life for every believer with benefits for you to enjoy. It is a place of community, spiritual growth, protection from false teaching, learning how to love others well, and using your spiritual gifts to help the body of Christ grow.

God knows you need the guidance of a pastor, the care of other Christians, and the safety and support of a good church community to help you grow as a Christian. Yet, no church is perfect just like no family is perfect. But a healthy church community is committed to these 4 things.

> **Worships Christ:** A healthy church presents Jesus as the Son of God and faith in Him alone as the only way to be saved from your sins and have a relationship with God.

> **Teaches His Word as truth:** A healthy church honors the Bible as God's Word, completely true, and the guidebook for life and decision-making.

> **Grows believers to follow Jesus together:** A healthy church encourages you to personally follow Jesus as His disciple and grow stronger in your faith just as we read in Ephesians chapter 4. When you are joined together with other believers who are growing in Christ, you each encourage one another and keep each other "fired up" in your mutual faith.

> **Encourages believers to proclaim the good news:** A healthy church is actively obeying Jesus' command in Matthew 28:19 to share the gospel with those who don't know Him yet. Look for a church that reaches out to non-Christians in your town.

Living as part of the church family is challenging.

Once you become part of a local church community, learning how to live as part of the family can be challenging. Jesus knows the difficulty we all have at times with one another. Your relationship with Him does not prevent you from misunderstandings or differences of opinion. Sometimes these relational challenges tempt you to harbor grudges against someone or to isolate yourself from the whole community. Neither of those is healthy for you. So you must be intentional in how you respond to people challenges in your church community.

> **Reconcile relationships quickly:** Jesus helped His disciples through their conflicts with one another. He told them to initiate reconciliation with a brother or sister that has something against you (Matthew 5:23-24). You are not responsible for the other person's response. You are responsible for your own efforts to initiate reconciliation. Pray for help to do your part and leave the rest in God's hands. You can say, "I can't, Jesus, but you can through me." And He will.

> **Stay connected:** One of the main reasons some Christians live defeated lives is that they have isolated themselves from other believers. Isolation will lead to stunted spiritual growth and a lack of joy in your life. Stay connected.

The treasure of the Church

You have a treasure in the Church as the Body of Christ. You can enjoy relationships and spiritual growth within this Church community (both local and universal). It is truly awesome to fellowship with others who love Christ and are living for Him!

Praise and thank God for adopting you into His family and giving you a community (the Body of Christ) in which to enjoy your life in Christ.

If you do not belong to a local church right now, ask Jesus to lead you to a church community where you can learn God's Word and continue to grow in your faith.

Let Jesus satisfy your heart with the confidence that the treasure you have in Him is more powerful and valuable than anything you could substitute for Him.

Reflect

Have you found a local church family? Thank God and ask Him how you can serve there.

Have you avoided involvement in a local church? Why? Ask Jesus to show you why you need a church family and to help you find the church community He wants you to join. He has promised to provide for you, so you can trust Him to answer your request.

Pray: Thank God for the treasure He has given you in Jesus Christ. Ask Him to help you recognize anything that you are substituting for Him. Ask Him to help you trust in Him alone for the power to be "successful" in life.

The Treasure of God's Empowering Presence

"Now to him who is able to do immeasurably more than all we ask or imagine, according to his power that is at work within us," (Ephesians 3:20, NIV)

> Pray: Lord Jesus, please teach me through this lesson.

As we study Ephesians, we are seeking the treasure we have in Jesus Christ. By faith in Him, we have the treasure of being rescued from darkness, receiving spectacular spiritual blessings, knowing we are dearly loved, and enjoying community in the awesome body of Christ.

All of these aspects of our treasure are evidence of God's spiritual power at work **for** us and **in** us. Because of that, we can live successfully in this world. God's Spirit power is greater than anything we could substitute for Him.

THE WORK OF THE HOLY SPIRIT

Our God is one God in three persons—Father God, His Son Jesus, and the Holy Spirit. The concept of the Holy Spirit's existence may seem like science fiction to you, like "the force is with you" from *Star Wars*. We often feel this way because His name is more like a title. With God the Father, we can relate to "father." With God the Son whose name is Jesus, we can relate to "son" and to "Jesus." As for the Holy Spirit, He is a personal being, not an impersonal "it" or simply an influence. In his letters, Paul helped us relate to Him by calling Him the Spirit of Christ or God's Spirit.

Once you believe in Christ, the Holy Spirit enters your spirit, makes you a new creation instantly possessing all those spiritual blessing jewels, and seals you with Himself so that your salvation is secure and guaranteed. He places you into the Body of Christ—the big "C" church. He does all those things to you whether you feel anything or not. As your **power** for spiritual life, He fills you with Himself and **transforms you from the inside out so that your character looks more like that of Jesus and your lifestyle glorifies God more than yourself.** The Holy Spirit is God's empowering presence at work in you—your power source for successful living.

Review Ephesians 3:16 and 20-21.

God's almighty power, greater than any other power anywhere, is **at work within us** through the Holy Spirit's empowering presence. Now, we usually think of external things when we consider this power that can do more than we ask or imagine—answered prayer for someone's healing, a new job, or freedom from an uncomfortable situation. But after Paul praised God (verse 21), the very next words have nothing to do with external things.

Write Ephesians 4:1 in the space below.

Although there is a chapter break here (added 1500 years after the letter was written), this is not a break in Paul's thoughts. It flows directly out of God's spiritual power at work within us and for the glory of Jesus Christ. Our calling is to be like Christ. This is both the goal of the Spirit's work within us and the choice we make to cooperate with Him. We are called to approach life God's way.

Paul's words implied there is another way, a substitute way of approaching life. We've seen that substitute way in Ephesians 2. The Bible calls it "living by the flesh." Unbelievers live by the flesh—doing what the flesh directs them to do, gratifying its cravings and following its desires and thoughts. Following the ways of this world also fits living by the flesh.

> The flesh is the personality of a human controlled by sin and directed to selfish pursuits rather than the service of God. (Dr. Charles Ryrie)

Basically, the flesh is the human in rebellion against God, coming from that part of the personality where sin dwells. That's why some translations use the phrase "sinful nature (NIV)" to describe the flesh.

We may not know what it is, but we definitely know how the flesh works. It sends enticing messages to your mind. These enticing messages get a lot of help from the world, which is influenced heavily by Satan (Ephesians 2:2). The work of the flesh is obvious. And it is ugly.

In Ephesians chapter 4, Paul gave us this great news: Believers don't have to live by the flesh.

PUT ON NEW CLOTHES

Read Ephesians 4:20-24.

What were the Ephesians taught regarding their former way of life (verse 22)?

What were the Ephesians taught about the new life available to them (verses 23-24)?

When you get new clothes or shoes to replace something old and worn, what do you most appreciate about having the new?

The former way of life was living by the flesh, gratifying its desires and cravings. Putting on the new self is a reference to your identity in Christ. But not only do we get a new identity in Christ when we believe, we also get an opportunity for new clothes. These are not made out of cloth or yarn but are new clothes for our minds and behavior.

But we must make the choice to put on those new clothes. Like old well-worn clothes, the old self doesn't improve over time. Yet, our choices can change over time as we learn to live by God's Spirit.

At the end of Ephesians chapter 3, Paul gave that fantastic declaration of God's immense power at work within us. He followed that with an appeal to live according to the new identity we have been given (Ephesians 4:1). Then, Paul began to address thoughts and behavior.

Read Ephesians 4:2-3.

Where do we start to begin living a life worthy of our new identity (verse 2, first part)?

Did this surprise you? Did you expect something more like "get rid of immorality, greed, and idolatry?"

Paul didn't start off with this humility and gentleness by accident. Humility is a decision you make to recognize God's authority over you and to desire what He wants more than what you want. You know that you've made that decision when you are willing to trust in God's goodness and accept His dealings with you as good without fighting Him on it.

Do you know how hard it is to be completely humble on your own? Sure, you do. Only God's Spirit power can make anyone completely humble!

In the Bible, humility is associated with gentleness. Gentleness carries the idea of strength under control. Whose strength? Your own! But choosing to put that strength under the Spirit's control instead is something only God's power can accomplish in us! Biblical gentleness—that strength under control—is a work of the Holy Spirit in your life. And it's the outworking of humility.

What comes after being completely humble and gentle (verses 2-3)?

Why would being humble and gentle make it easier for you to do those?

Those first few verses of chapter 4 are the foundation of living by Spirit power in critical areas of life. If you start with being completely humble and gentle, you can do everything else that follows in Ephesians 4, 5, and 6!

After Paul wrote in verses 22-24 about putting off the old self and putting on the new self, he gave some examples of what that looks like. He basically answered the question, "How do you know if you are living by Spirit power or by your flesh power?"

Consider our analogy of changing your clothes to a new wardrobe. Ephesians 4:25-32 are contrasts between the old clothes and the new clothes. Every piece of the old clothing is a substitute power.

Read Ephesians 4:25.

What is the old to put off?

What is the new to put on?

Why?

Read Ephesians 4:26-27.

What is the old to put off?

What is the new to put on? (Hint: opposite of holding onto anger)

Why?

Read Ephesians 4:28.

What is the old to put off?

What is the new to put on?

Why?

Read Ephesians 4:29.

What is the old to put off?

What is the new to put on?

Why?

Read Ephesians 4:31-32.

What is the old to put off?

What is the new to put on?

Why?

Did you notice all the substitute powers? Lying, holding onto anger, stealing, hurtful words, rage, bitterness, and slander. All of those are substitute powers you can rely upon to get your way. All of those are substitutes for trusting God and His goodness to you.

Considering what you have learned so far in Ephesians, why should you want to change clothes and who would benefit from your doing so?

YOUR TREASURE IN CHRIST

These new behaviors do not come naturally to anyone and so are hard to consistently do. You can probably remember to act that way once in a while on your own but not all the time. It's only possible on a consistent basis because you have God's empowering presence in you. He is ready and able to transform you. He enables you to live God's way as you trust Him to work in and through you. By faith, you can access His power to help you.

As long as you live in your earthly body, you will be tempted to sin. Sin will happen—whether intentionally or unintentionally.

Do you recognize that you are living by the flesh in one of those ways described in Ephesians 4:25-32?

Do you want to change and put on new clothes in that area?

If your answer is yes, follow this biblical process for dealing with recognized sin as a believer:

➢ View yourself rightly through your identity in Christ (Ephesians 1:4-14).

➢ Agree with God that you are guilty of that behavior. That's confession. You are already forgiven (Ephesians 1:7).

➢ Choose obedience and decide you want to live by the Spirit's power in that area of your life. That's repentance.

➢ Depend on the Spirit's power by saying, *"Lord Jesus, I can't do _____ on my own, but you can do _____ in my life. I trust your Spirit to do this in me."* Watch what He does!

> **After all the lessons, you will find this biblical process with additional explanation. Take a picture and keep it handy.**

Submitting to your own flesh power always leads away from God's way of approaching life to your own way or the world's way. Living by Spirit power always leads to God's way of approaching life.

Spiritual growth involves Jesus continually teaching you to trust Him in new or unexplored areas of your life. The treasure you have in Jesus Christ is more powerful and valuable than anything you could substitute for Him.

DEPEND ON THE TREASURE OF GOD'S EMPOWERING PRESENCE

Recommended: Listen to the podcast "DEPEND ON THE TREASURE OF GOD'S EMPOWERING PRESENCE." Use the section below as a listener guide.

The Holy Spirit is God's empowering presence in your life. And this great power, which can do more than we ask or imagine, is **at work within you** to do the work God wants done in your life.

Our calling is to be like Christ. So the Holy Spirit fills you with Himself and transforms you from the inside out so that your character begins to look more like that of Jesus and your lifestyle glorifies God more than yourself. To be like Christ means that you approach life God's way. Yet, there is a substitute way for approaching life. You saw that substitute way in Ephesians 2. The Bible calls it "living by the flesh."

Living by the flesh is a substitute way of approaching life.

The flesh is the personality of a human controlled by sin and directed to selfish pursuits rather than the service of God. When you were saved, your spirit was given new life. But you are still living in the old body with your original personality. Your mind, emotions, and will are part of that original personality and are still influenced by that sinful nature.

The flesh does not improve or change its nature over time, and it gets a lot of help from the world, which is influenced heavily by Satan (Ephesians 2:2). Flesh power is strong. It always leads *away* from God's way of approaching life to your own way or the world's way. The result is ugly.

Paul described some of this ugliness in Ephesians chapter 4: lying, stealing, holding onto anger, speaking hurtful words, harboring bitterness and unforgiveness, exhibiting rage and meanness in word and action.

Believers don't have to live by the flesh.

But here's the great news. You are not helpless against your flesh that is always trying to make you sin against God. God rescued you from being in bondage to sin by placing Himself inside you. You don't have to live by the flesh. God's empowering presence living inside is greater than the substitute power of your flesh. The Spirit gives you the ability to overcome the power of the flesh within you and to choose a new way of thinking and a new way of living.

This new way of living is called "living by the Spirit." Living by the Spirit begins with desiring God's way over your own way. It's lived out as you submit to God's Spirit to help you daily live out the life of Christ within you. For every situation you face, begin with this question, "What does God want me to do versus what do I want or feel like doing?" As you study the Scriptures, you will discover God's way for everything.

You will be transformed step by step as the Spirit reveals to you where you need to change your way of thinking or living. Over time, you will recognize that you are living by the Spirit in some areas of your life while living by the flesh in others. As you grow in your faith, Jesus will teach you to trust Him in new or unexplored areas of your life. The result is that you will be approaching life God's way more and more.

Living by the Spirit is God's way of approaching life.

> *"Be completely humble and gentle; be patient, bearing with one another in love. Make every effort to keep the unity of the Spirit through the bond of peace." (Ephesians 4:2-3)*

Overcoming the power of your flesh begins with humility and gentleness. Humility is a decision you make to recognize God's authority over you and desire what He wants more than what you want. You know that you've made that decision when you are willing to trust in God's goodness and accept His dealings with you as good without fighting Him on it.

Gentleness carries the idea of strength under control. You and I have the strength in our flesh to crush the spirit of someone, to cuss out, to cheat, to lie, and to steal. But choosing to put that strength under the Spirit's control instead is something **only God's power can accomplish in us!** And it's the outworking of humility.

When you start with humility and gentleness, then you can be patient with people and situations because you are trusting God about them. You can lovingly bear with other believers because that's what God does as He bears with your mistakes and quirkiness. You can be one who unites more than divides in your local church community. This is not ignoring real issues that must be addressed. It is more along the lines of not being picky, critical, and more interested in pleasing your own preferences rather than magnifying Christ. Living by Spirit power will promote unity.

Starting with the foundation of humility, gentleness, patience, bearing with one another, and keeping the unity of the Spirit gives you a basis to deal with two of the most challenging situations we face in relationships: anger and hurtful words. Both of these are substitute powers.

Overcoming 2 substitute powers—anger and hurtful speech

You and I both know that anger is a powerful force. We also know that not all anger is bad because God expresses the emotion of anger, and Christ felt anger in His time on earth (Mark 3:1-5). God's anger is directed against sin and the hurt that sin causes. That's called righteous anger. But remember that God also describes Himself as "compassionate and gracious, slow to anger, and abounding in lovingkindness and truth" (Exodus 34:6-7). God's anger is always under control, and He takes action when needed.

God has given humans the emotion of anger. Its purpose is to alert us to something that requires appropriate action. So what should you do for any situation that stirs anger in you? First, ask yourself this question, "Why am I angry? What appropriate action should I take?"

The problem for us is that rarely does our anger stay righteous like God's for very long before our sinful nature takes over. That's why we need to deal with it quickly and get rid of it (Ephesians 4:26-27). Sinful anger leads to broken relationships. The action to take is reconciliation. Any time you give the devil a foothold in a relationship, you are giving way to a substitute for trusting God.

Whenever you recognize unresolved anger, rage, and bitterness in yourself, you know you are living by the flesh rather than by the Spirit. It's like pH paper reveals an acid or base.

That is true not only about your angry behavior but also the hurtful words that you say, especially when you are angry or disappointed.

> *"Do not let any unwholesome talk come out of your mouths, but only what is helpful for building others up according to their needs, that it may benefit those who listen." (Ephesians 4:29)*

Think about what you say to those around you and how you respond to them. Ask yourself: "What did I say that was building them up and beneficial to them? Or am I just blowing off steam in a mean way?" Maybe you have fallen into a bad habit of mean words. Stop it. If a believer is mean to you, quote Ephesians 4:29 and say, "Want to try that again?"

It's so easy to blame people or circumstances for our anger. Yes, what people do can stir up anger. But people and circumstances do not make you impatient, hold onto bitterness, or fly into fits of rage. They don't make you speak hurtful words. Your reactions to people and circumstances usually reveal where you are living—by God's empowering presence or by your own flesh power.

The answer is to go back to what you need to do to live a life worthy of the Lord. As Paul wrote in Ephesians 4:31-32, put off bitterness, rage, anger, brawling, slander, and malice; put on kindness, compassion, and forgiveness. In fact, you are called to be as forgiving as God. Only God's Spirit power can make you **that** forgiving! He will help you find scriptures that deal with that issue and will lead you back to trusting God with that situation and the results.

Resisting the treasure of God's empowering presence

But what if you don't want to change and would rather live by the flesh in a few areas and resist God's empowering presence in you? You need to know a few things about choosing that way:

➢ Submitting to the flesh always leads away from God's way of approaching life to your own way or the world's way.

➢ Because of your faith in Christ, God's grace is continually forgiving you of sin. But you don't have permission to intentionally sin without consequences.

➢ You are free to choose to sin, but you are not free to choose when or how the consequences of that sinful behavior will hurt you or will hurt those you love.

➢ Pursuing a sinful lifestyle as a believer does not change your identity. But it does change your usefulness to God and definitely the enjoyment of your spiritual blessing jewels in Christ. You will not be living successfully as a believer in Christ and definitely not worthy of your calling.

The Holy Spirit is God's power source for successful living

God takes our rubbish and turns it into treasure. He says, "Look what I can do in a human life." Do you want to live successfully? You can live successfully in the power already available to you through God's Spirit who is greater than anything you could substitute for Him. That's the treasure of God's empowering presence.

Let Jesus satisfy your heart with the confidence that the treasure you have in Him is more powerful and valuable than anything you could substitute for Him.

Reflect

We cannot see the Holy Spirit inside of us. But we know He is working inside us because we become aware of the evidence. These are some of the things the Spirit does for us:

> ➤ He helps us understand what the Bible teaches.

> ➤ He gives us the words to tell others about Jesus and say that Jesus is God.

> ➤ He gives us assurance that we are God's children.

> ➤ He makes us want to do what pleases God.

> ➤ He helps us feel joy as we serve Jesus and when we do the right things.

> ➤ He makes us not want to do what doesn't please God.

> ➤ He makes us to become more like Jesus, especially in loving other people.

> ➤ He makes us want to sing praises to God, in our hearts and out loud, and be thankful for God's goodness.

> ➤ He prays for us when we need help or don't know how to pray.

Which of these evidences have you recognized in your life? Thank God for specific ways and times His Spirit has worked in your life. Ask Him to make you more aware of His empowering presence in you.

Find a more detailed description of this at the end of this book.

Pray: Thank God for the treasure He has given you in Jesus Christ. Ask Him to help you recognize anything that you are substituting for Him. Ask Him to help you trust in Him alone for the power to be "successful" in life.

The Treasure of Godliness

"and to put on the new self, created to be like God in true righteousness and holiness." (Ephesians 4:24, NIV)

Pray: Lord Jesus, please teach me through this lesson.

God's power at work within us can do immeasurably more than all we can ask or imagine for Him to do. He works within us to change us from the inside out. His goal is to make our thoughts, behavior, and words match up to who we are in Christ. In the first words of Ephesians 5, Paul gave us the reason why we should want this and the basis for making those changes in our lives.

Read Ephesians 5:1-2.

Whose examples are we to follow and how?

We've already basked in the treasure of being dearly loved by God. So now let's focus on the first part of verse 1. "Follow God's example." Following God's example of sacrificial love and choosing to live life His way leads to something called godliness. **Godliness is devotion to God expressed in a life that is pleasing to Him.**

The word devotion means profound dedication, earnest attachment to a cause or person. So devotion to God means you are dedicated to Him. You are firmly attached to Him. Whatever He wants, you want. It is a loyal love for God. Godliness begins with that.

But it's not just a warm, emotional feeling about God that you get when you have personal Bible reading and prayer or when you sing worship songs. Godliness is devotion in action. Something results from that devotion. Your loyal love for God expresses itself in a life that reflects His character and who He is. This is your new self, to be like God (Ephesians 4:24), and is embodied in the word godliness. Because we have the Spirit of God within us, godliness is possible. Living a life of godliness is another treasure for us.

Paul gave us examples in chapter 4 of what godliness looks like and what it doesn't look like. He gave us more in chapter 5.

WHAT GODLINESS DOESN'T LOOK LIKE

Read Ephesians 5:3.

What ungodly behaviors should not be associated with you as a Christian?

Why?

Sexual immorality is any sex outside of marital sex between a man and a woman. Impurity refers to any kind of moral filthiness. That includes lying, stealing, and giving way to anger and rage. It also includes having a heart that promotes active rebellion against God. Greed is a desire to have more stuff and includes coveting what others have. Sexual immorality, moral impurity, and greed are the opposite of our God's sacrificial love for us (verse 1) and certainly not evidence of following Him or being like Him.

Read Ephesians 5:4.

What ungodly words should not be associated with you as a Christian?

Obscenity is sexually suggestive talk including vulgar jokes. That kind of talk, like gossip, is neither building others up nor benefiting those who listen (Ephesians 4:29). Foolish talk refers to stupid words that waste time saying them. Coarse joking refers to humorous insults and talk that damages someone's reputation. It is not general joking. There's nothing wrong with a good laugh at something harmlessly funny. God has a sense of humor and gave it to us. Obscenity, foolish talk, and coarse joking are substitutes for sacrificial love.

If you say such ungodly words, why do you?

With what should you replace them? Why would thanksgiving be a good replacement for obscenity, foolish talk, and coarse joking?

A life of godliness is not a life of sexual immorality, impurity, greed, obscenity, coarse joking, and rebellion against God. In verse 5, Paul called these bad behaviors "idols." An idol is any human-created God substitute. It's what the world says guarantees success—sex, money, and power. But they are totally wrong for God's dearly loved children. They are the opposite of being completely humble, gentle, and imitating God in sacrificial love. They are the opposite of godliness.

The rest of Ephesians chapter 5 and the first part of chapter 6 describe what a life of godliness looks like.

WHAT GODLINESS LOOKS LIKE

Read Ephesians 5:8-10.

As one who has been rescued from darkness by faith in Christ, how are you to live (verse 8)?

What three things characterize those who live as children of the light (verse 9)?

Children of the light intentionally do what (verse 10)?

Children of the light live in devotion to the God who rescued them from the darkness. A life of godliness is expressed in doing that which is good and right in God's eyes as well as firmly grasping God's truth. You can find God's truth in the Bible. It's there for you to know it. And it's where you will find what pleases the Lord as you choose a life of godliness.

Read Ephesians 5:15-18.

A life of godliness makes intentional choices every day whether to follow the ways of the world or God's way.

According to verses 15-16, what choices must you make?

That phrase "the days are evil" refers to the influence of the world on your mind and behavior.

According to verse 17, what choice must you make?

According to verse 18, what choice must you make?

Those are all choices of obedience. Be careful how you live. Recognize the evils. Live wisely and not foolishly. Understand what God's will is for you, which is clearly revealed throughout the book of Ephesians and the rest of the New Testament. And choose God's Spirit power over any other power in your life.

The concept of being filled with God is connected to all of Ephesians. Jesus Christ wants you to be filled with Himself (Ephesians 1:23; 3:19) so that He is the dominating power behind your thoughts, words, and behavior (Ephesians 3:17). When you submit to Christ as Lord and desire to obey Him more than your flesh, the Spirit fills you with power and strength to do that (Ephesians 3:16). It is a choice of obedience to Christ, not some mystical experience.

The filling of the Spirit is not a stand-alone verse. It is connected to all of chapter 4 and verses 1-17 of chapter five. Paul took something from his culture which if done in excess will take control over your behavior from the inside and produce behavior that is the opposite of godliness. He compared being filled with the Spirit to drunkenness. So "filling" is a metaphor (picture) of control by an internal influence. It's still an issue of power.

As you live the Christian life, face temptations, and make decisions, the Spirit will transform your life to become more like that of Christ as you are depending on Him to do that. And godliness is the fruit of being filled by the Spirit rather than being filled with the flesh or anything the world has to offer. Being filled with the Spirit is living by the Spirit, an ongoing choice you must continually make.

When you are devoted to God and live in a way that pleases Him, that will flow from you in recognizable ways. We've already seen a few of those in Ephesians 4 and 5—humility, gentleness, love, forgiveness, patience, kindness, compassion, and choosing right over wrong.

Read Ephesians 5:19-20.

Godliness expresses itself in what ways?

Godliness expresses itself in worship, a joyful heart, and being thankful to God for **everything**. Only God's Spirit power can make you **that** thankful!

GODLINESS IS LIVED OUT IN OUR RELATIONSHIPS.

The rest of Ephesians chapter 5 and the first half of chapter 6 are examples of how godliness is lived out in relationships with others, especially other Christians.

Read Ephesians 5:21.

As believers, we are to do what and why?

Submission is voluntary yielding to another. It flows from humility and gentleness, the first characteristics of godliness that we saw in Ephesians 4:2. Jesus Christ is our example of submission (Ephesians 5:2). His sacrificial love for us submitted to our needs over His own. And He submitted to His Father's will as He "gave himself up for us as a fragrant offering and sacrifice to God." Submission to one another is evidence of trusting God rather than forcing your own way over others.

The next verses are addressed to Christians wanting to live God's way in family relationships through submission to God and sacrificial love.

Read Ephesians 5:22-33.

Focus on the wife's choices in verses 22-24, 33:

How would this behavior reflect Christ submission to His Father?

How would this behavior reflect Christ's sacrificial love?

Focus on the husband's choices in verses 25-29, 33:

How would this behavior reflect Christ's submission to His Father?

How would this behavior reflect Christ's sacrificial love?

Read Ephesians 6:1-4.

In what ways would the children's choices reflect Christ's submission to His Father (verse 1)?

In what ways would parents' choices reflect Christ's sacrificial love (verse 4)?

Reflecting both Christ's submission to His Father and His sacrificial love for humans requires trusting God in all these family interactions. None of this comes naturally or is easy to do. When you start with your devotion to God and your willingness to obey Him above your own inclinations, the result will be godliness in your family relationships.

Read Ephesians 6:5-9.

Being an indentured servant or slave was a common experience for Christians in Ephesus. The Bible doesn't condone the practice of slavery. Wherever the gospel has taken hold, the institution of slavery has been abolished in most of the world. The counsel for the master / slave relationship was in the context of a work place. Households were work places. Slaves worked for masters. Masters managed and determined work tasks for workers in their households—both slave and free. All Christian slaves or masters were to adorn themselves with godliness as individuals.

In what ways would the workers' choices reflect Christ's submission to His Father (verses 5-8)?

In what ways would the managers' choices reflect Christ's sacrificial love (verse 9)?

Godliness is a treasure you have because of God's empowering presence in you. It results from yielding to the Spirit's work in your life. It requires trusting God more than your own natural inclinations. And godliness adds more value to your life and relationships than anything the world has to offer.

YOUR TREASURE IN CHRIST

The power for joyful, successful living is already available to you through God's Spirit and leads you to the treasure of godliness, which is more valuable than anything you can substitute for it.

What have you allowed to have power or influence over you more than your devotion to God? Think addictions, work, digital media, binging on alcohol or television, obsession about your looks, immorality, greed, ungodly words, or something else.

How has that shown up in your relationships?

Are you willing to let go of those other influencers? If so, you can say, "Lord Jesus, I can't let go of _____ on my own. I need your Spirit's help to do this in me. I will trust in you to work in my life." Then, watch what He does!

LIVE OUT THE TREASURE OF GODLINESS

Recommended: *Listen to the podcast "LIVE OUT THE TREASURE OF GODLINESS." Use the section below as a listener guide.*

SEEK THE TREASURE

> Godliness is devotion to God expressed in a life that is pleasing to Him.

Devotion to God begins with loving Him so much that you want to please Him with your life. The first half of Paul's letter was filled with reasons why you should devote yourself to God and love Him wholeheartedly. He rescued you from the spiritual darkness that kept you separated from Him. He saved you because of His great love for you. God filled your spiritual treasure chest with amazing blessing jewels you have in Christ. He wants you to know Him intimately and to know that you are dearly loved. How can anyone not respond with love and gratitude for what He has done!

Devotion to God is not cold and austere. It's not living a life that is boring, colorless, and serious all the time. It isn't a life without laughter or pleasure. Those are not biblical descriptions of devotion to God.

Look at Jesus. He celebrated weddings with His family. He went on retreats to the mountains with His disciples. He ate meals in the homes of friends and foes. He radiated the joy of the Lord. He was not cold and austere.

Devotion to God is also not just living by a set of rules. God isn't interested in outward conformity. He had enough of that with the Jews in the Old Testament. God doesn't just want us to act properly. He's interested in our hearts first. When our hearts are right, we will want to obey Him with our thinking and behavior. We will want to reflect Him well because we love Him so much. It's that loyal love for Him. Godliness begins in the heart and mind then is lived out in words and behavior.

Adorning yourself with godliness

The Bible uses the image of adorning yourself with godliness. That fits in with Paul's use of taking off old clothes and putting on new and better ones. We as women like to adorn ourselves with clothes that reflect who we are. We discard the ones that don't fit, that are the wrong color, and that are stained or torn. We get new ones that fit us well, that complement our appearance, and fulfill a purpose. That same concept applies to adorning ourselves with godliness.

You express your devotion to God by taking on His likeness—Godlikeness, not becoming God but presenting Him. As you learned in the last lesson, His empowering presence in you has given you everything you need to be able to do this. But there is even more help for you—the example of Jesus (Ephesians 5:1-2).

Jesus is your example of godliness as a human. As you read through the four books that tell of the life of Jesus—Matthew, Mark, Luke, and John, you get to know Jesus well and see His example of what godliness looks like.

Jesus adorned Himself with godliness through humility, compassion, love, prayer, dependency on God the Father, good works, and many more ways. All those pointed to a God who was good and worthy of your devotion. Jesus loved His Father and felt His Father's love. He submitted to His Father's will. His words were in line with His Father's words. His devotion to God was expressed in a life that reflected God and was pleasing to God.

The best way to understand godliness is to look at the contrast between what godliness looks like and what it doesn't look like. Paul gave us examples in chapter 4 of what godliness looks like and what it doesn't look like. He gave us more in chapter 5.

The stained clothes of ungodliness

A life that is devoted to God is not identified by sexual immorality, moral filthiness, or greed. Our culture deceives us into thinking that living a moral life as a Christian is unimportant or impossible. Christian women and men are having sex outside of marriage at the same rate as the unbelieving world does. Why? It's because we aren't convinced that it matters. We get content living by the flesh. We like to do what we feel like doing rather than what God wants us to do.

That is true also about the words from our mouths that are associated with immorality and greed—obscenity, foolish talk, and coarse joking. Has this type of talk been your habit? Evaluate for yourself what this is. It is living by flesh power and the opposite of godliness. Stop it! Follow the biblical process for dealing with recognized sin you learned in Lesson 6.

Paul also cautioned believers about the bad influence of people who are against God and living that out in their lives (Ephesians 5:7). Paul basically said, "Have nothing to do with their behavior" (Ephesians 5:11). Rather, bring that ungodly behavior to light by calling it what it is—sin!

You as a believer can never be separated from the life of God because the Spirit of God is in you forever, But you can be influenced by ungodly people to harden your own heart towards God. You can lose sensitivity to the Spirit's work in your life. As you learned in the last lesson, you can choose to give yourself over to sensuality as the unbelievers do by their sinful nature. Paul wrote in 1 Corinthians 15:33, "Bad company corrupts good character." You've seen that happen so you know it is true.

So the Bible tells believers to not be partners with those who are in rebellion against God. That's not who you are now. Your new identity is in Christ. You have been rescued from the kingdom of darkness and are now in God's light. Paul wrote in Ephesians 5:8, live as children of the light. Don't join with them so that your life looks like theirs. Their influence does not contribute to your godliness.

A life of godliness is not a life of sexual immorality, impurity, greed, obscenity, coarse joking, and rebellion against God. The rest of Ephesians chapter 5 and the first part of chapter 6 describe what a life of godliness looks like—that new self, created to be like God (Ephesians 4:24).

The new clothes of godliness

A life of godliness is expressed in doing what is right in God's eyes, and firmly grasping God's truth. It makes intentional choices every day to follow God's ways rather than the world's ways. It is seeking to understand what God's will is for you, as clearly revealed throughout the book of Ephesians and the rest of the New Testament. And godliness chooses God's Spirit power over any other power in your life. Doing that leads to being filled with the Spirit.

What is this filling of the Spirit? As we have learned in Ephesians, every person who trusts in Christ receives the Holy Spirit so that He is **with you** and **in you** forever. You have all of Him, not part of Him. Being filled with the Spirit is not getting more of the Spirit inside of you. It is also not something magical or mystical. You won't hear any kind of gong when you are filled with the Spirit.

The filling of the Spirit occurs when you choose to be more influenced by Christ than by yourself or anything else. As we have seen in Ephesians 1 and 3, Christ wants to fill you with Himself. He can do this as you choose obedience to God and His ways in all those areas of life described in Ephesians 4, 5 and 6. Godliness is the fruit of being filled by the Spirit rather than being filled with the flesh or anything the world has to offer.

What powers are you letting control you? We look at alcohol or substance abuse and easily recognize those controls. But what about other things that take control of us and produce not-so-good results? You and I can become addicted to social media, shopping, and gambling. We can also become addicted to work, filled with an obsession to work, producing stress and neglect of family. We can be filled and controlled by fleshly desires (like what alcohol does), or we can be filled and controlled by the Spirit. Those are the choices.

Being filled with God's Spirit is an issue of power. We can be too full of substitute powers. I'll go back to my earlier question. What things have you allowed to have influence over you? What have you embraced as a substitute for Christ? Ask Him to give you the strength to let it go. When you yield to Him, He will fill you with His Spirit and help you learn how to let go of those other influencers.

Pursue the treasure of godliness.

Pursuing godliness requires making choices. It may seem like hard work to recognize the wrong influences in your life and delete them from having power over you. So why do it? I can think of at least three reasons why you and I should pursue godliness in our lives.

> ➢ Pursue godliness **for God the Father and the Lord Jesus Christ** because of your love for them and gratitude for what they have done for your salvation.

> ➢ Pursue godliness **for yourself and your fellow Christians** because godly behavior is good for you in every way.

> ➢ Pursue godliness **for others who are watching** because godliness makes the teaching about Christ attractive and draws unbelievers to the God you know and serve.

When you choose daily to yield to the Spirit's influence over your own self-dependence, the Holy Spirit fills you with spiritual power so that Christ is the dominating factor over your thoughts, words, and behavior. As you approach life God's way, you will please God and become the visible representation of the invisible God to those who are watching. It's a win/win.

But your willingness to let Spirit power control and transform you requires you to recognize that you are weak to do anything of spiritual significance on your own. That goes against the western mindset that you must be strong on your own, stand on your own two feet. But your weakness is more useful to God than your self-determined strength.

The power for joyful, successful living is already available to you through God's Spirit and leads you to live out the treasure of godliness in your life every day.

Let Jesus satisfy your heart with the confidence that the treasure you have in Him is more powerful and valuable than anything you could substitute for Him.

Reflect

When you are devoted to God and live in a way that pleases Him, that will flow from you in recognizable ways. How have you seen this to be true?

Pray: Thank God for the treasure He has given you in Jesus Christ. Ask Him to help you recognize anything that you are substituting for Him. Ask Him to help you trust in Him alone for the power to be "successful" in life.

The Treasure of Victory in Christ

"Finally, be strong in the Lord and in His mighty power." (Ephesians 6:10, NIV)

Pray: Lord Jesus, please teach me through this lesson.

Throughout this study, we have learned about the power of God at work in and for us as believers. We've learned the difference between spiritual power as described by the Bible and what the world seeks for "spiritual" power—formulas that guarantee success, lucky shirts and caps, bead necklaces, or an energy field connecting nature.

The Bible says we have a personal God who uses His power to accomplish His own will and purposes. He extends that power to those who trust in Him to accomplish His will and purposes in their lives, also. God extends His power to those He loves. That's why it is based on faith, not on formulas or lucky charms or bead necklaces.

That truth permeates the whole letter to the Ephesians. God's power **for** us is used to take care of us and to change us from the inside out as we trust Him. We can live successfully in the power already available to us through God's Spirit who is greater than anything we could substitute for Him.

That applies to daily life and relationships when it comes to dealing with our own selfishness or the selfishness of others. We can have victory over the flesh through the power of the Spirit in us moving us to do the right thing and producing godliness in our lives.

Some challenges that come against us can't be explained by selfish human behavior as much as by an unseen enemy controlling people or situations. These are spiritual battles against evil forces working against us. We can have victory during spiritual battles through the power of Jesus Christ.

Read Ephesians 1:19-23.

Jesus is at the right hand of God with everything under His feet. Anything competing with Jesus for power over you or that you might turn to as a source of power is nothing compared to Jesus. All substitute powers are there under His feet. That would include all the angels and demons and Satan himself. That would include every idol, every name or formula used to defeat your enemy, and traditions that seem to work to give you success at what you want or need.

Believers are under His head as the body of Christ. We are not under His feet. That's where our enemies are. And Christ fills us with everything we need for spiritual life and victory over anything that comes against us. There's nothing lacking. We are prepared to go forth.

We will have trouble in this world because evil still exists until Christ returns. Paul told the Ephesians and us how to overcome bad things by trusting in the power of Christ to hold onto us and protect us. We are given God's very armor to wear during the battle—more new clothing for us. All of this is ours. We just need to use it.

Read Ephesians 6:10-13.

Write verse 10 in the space below.

Why put on the full armor of God (verse 11)?

Who is against you (verse 12)?

What will you be able to do because of the armor (verse 13)?

From what you've learned, how can you be strong in the Lord?

The power of the Spirit helps you overcome the power of your flesh (your sinful nature). But you have two other enemies—Satan and his demons plus the world system which is under the devil's power. Because of that, there are things going on around us that we cannot see. There is a battle going on, largely invisible, but it affects our world. We can see the evidence of that. And the Church is a target for our spiritual enemies. Why is that?

Read Ephesians 3:10.

Through whom is God's wisdom made known to that invisible world?

The Church is God's display of His wisdom to the angels, both the good and bad ones (demons). We are trophies of Jesus' victory over sin and death. But the evil forces haven't quit waging war against God in heaven or on earth. They don't like losing influence, so they come after us.

We are on God's side. They are at war against God. We become part of the battle. We know the ending, though. God's side wins. In the work of Christ, the victory has been clinched.

But for this ongoing battle, Jesus clothes you and me with armor that He has provided. The armor that Christ provides for you isn't real armor. It's things you know to be true—spiritual armor. Christ gives you this armor so you can stand strong whenever you are attacked or tested. By using this armor, you learn to trust in Christ's power rather than in your own. Using this armor will enable you to stand firm and not give way to the enemy, fear, or substitute powers when you are afraid. It is God's armor. He's already given it to you. You just need to acknowledge it and use it.

In Ephesians chapter 6, Paul described God's armor, using the image of a Roman soldier fully prepared for battle.

Read Ephesians 6:14-18.

In verse 14, what two pieces of armor have you been given?

In verse 15, what piece of armor have you been given?

In verse 16, what piece of armor have you been given?

In verse 17, what two pieces of armor have you been given?

In verse 18, what privilege have you been given to communicate with your commanding general (God)?

For a battle-ready Roman soldier, all the pieces of armor worked together to protect the soldier during battle. The same is true for you. The soldier's belt held his weapons so your belt is the truth of God's Word. Your breastplate is forgiveness of sin and Christ's righteousness covering you and protecting you from the devil's accusations about your sin. Your shoes are the truth of the gospel that you can share with others so they can have peace with God too. Your shield is your faith in the truth that God always loves you and is always with you. Your helmet is your secure salvation by faith in Christ. Your sword is God's Word and the Spirit of God working in you.

Prayer is your freedom to talk to God in fearful situations and trust Him to do amazing things on your behalf. Nothing is too big or impossible with prayer because God can do anything that He wants to do. He will answer the way He knows is best. So pray in the Spirit, by the Spirit, and through the Spirit—God's empowering presence within you. Prayer is an act of faith in Jesus as the greater power.

All those things listed as the armor of God come in one bundle along with those spiritual blessing jewels you discovered in Ephesians 1:3-14. You got those because you are in Christ. Protection comes from what God has already provided you to use. Acknowledge and use it.

Review Ephesians 6:11-16.

What are you able to do with God's armor (verses 11, 13, 14)?

What would it look like to stand firm?

What would be the opposite?

What are you also able to do (verse 16)?

What could the "flaming arrows of the evil one" coming against you look like?

Flaming arrows thrown at you are anything meant to deceive you to move away from trusting God, to be self-sufficient rather than God-dependent, to feel helpless and hopeless, and to make you rely on substitute powers.

What God has already provided is completely sufficient to extinguish all those flaming arrows thrown at you. By faith in Jesus as the greater power, the fiery darts of deception, doubt, despair, mistrust, hopelessness, and helplessness will be extinguished as they hit your firm faith in Jesus. Stand firm in the fact that you are a child of God, one of His saints, dearly loved and accepted by God. You are in Christ. Nothing or no one is more powerful than He is. He is **for you!**

Are you confident in that?

Trust Jesus' power to protect you and bring good into your life rather than any lucky socks, prayer formulas, or statues. He is greater than diplomas, social status, gazillions of dollars, or your own self-reliance. There may be evil spiritual forces behind the people, the habits, and the situations that are messing up your life. But the answer is not to try out everything available to see if something sticks. You don't need substitute power. **The treasure you have in Jesus Christ is more powerful than anything you could substitute for Him**.

Believe that in your head and in your heart. Get rid of anything else you might be relying upon for spiritual power. Trust in what you already have in Jesus. Live every day in that power.

YOUR TREASURE IN CHRIST

Reflect on the song lyrics below.

You hear me when I call. You are my morning song. Though darkness fills the night, it cannot hide the light. Whom shall I fear.

You crush the enemy underneath my feet. You are my sword and shield though troubles linger still. Whom shall I fear.

My strength is in Your name for You alone can save. You will deliver me. Yours is the victory. Whom shall I fear.

I know Who goes before me. I know Who stands behind. The God of angel armies is always by my side. The One who reigns forever, He is a Friend of mine. The God of angel armies is always by my side.

And nothing formed against me shall stand. You hold the whole world in Your hands. I'm holding onto Your promises. You are faithful; you are faithful. ("Whom Shall I Fear" by Chris Tomlin)

Respond with a declaration of your own trust in Christ for protection against anything.

STAND FIRM IN THE TREASURE OF VICTORY IN CHRIST

Recommended: *Listen to the podcast "STAND FIRM IN THE TREASURE OF VICTORY IN CHRIST." Use the section below as a listener guide.*

Spiritual warfare is real. It has two aspects: 1) that which is taking place in the heavenly realms and 2) that which involves attacks against Christians on earth.

Spiritual warfare in the heavenly realms

There is a battle raging in heaven between God and His angels versus Satan and his underlings, the demons. Satan is not the equal of God. He is a created being just like every other angel. Yet, he chose to lead a rebellion against God that is continuing to this day.

The Bible teaches that God has imprisoned some of the demons while allowing others to roam freely. Yet, we see in the Gospels that they are still under the authority of Christ. We are to be aware of this, but it is not our concern. Nothing you or I can do will make a difference in that invisible heavenly battle.

Spiritual warfare against us

When that heavenly battle affects our world, then it involves us. The devil with his demons influence the world system, which is under their power. But that's not enough. They target the Church with what Paul called "the flaming arrows of the evil one" in Ephesians 6:16. Why do they target the Church? We are on God's side. They are at war against God.

Just because bad things happen in this fallen world, know that they are not all caused by demons. Having an unhealthy focus on demons can be dangerous and distracting from following Christ. You should know that demons exist and be aware of their deceptive nature. Jesus is greater than all demons, and He lives in you. Demons have no authority over you. You have nothing to fear. Focus on Jesus, not demons.

The evil forces don't like losing influence. So they come after us. We become part of the battle. We know the ending, though. God's side wins. In the work of Christ, the victory has been clinched. And the power and position of our Lord Jesus Christ over all of His enemies guarantees our victory as well. Anything competing with Jesus for power over you or that you might turn to as a source of power is nothing compared to Jesus.

Jesus fills you with everything you need for spiritual life. There's nothing lacking. And you are prepared and ready to go forth because our God has clothed you with His armor.

Clothed with the armor of God

Did you know that God has armor? He doesn't need it. But He puts it on when He means business. God Himself puts on a breastplate of righteousness and a helmet of salvation to fight battles for His people (Isaiah 59:17). Isn't that a comforting picture?

> "No, in all these things we are more than conquerors through him who loved us." (Romans 8:37)

So when Paul wrote Ephesians 6:10-18, he pictured God putting His armor on us. We wear it because we are in Christ. God's armor will enable us to stand firm and not give way to any substitute powers because we are afraid. It is God's armor. He's already put it on us. We just need to acknowledge it and use it. The struggle is for faith in an unseen God to defeat an unseen enemy. Protection comes from what God has provided.

Stand firm against the fiery darts of the devil.

Spiritual warfare is primarily waged over truth and error. The battleground is your mind. Satan's weapons are lies aimed to produce deception, fear, and despair. His strategy, as we saw in Ephesians 2, is to hinder people from coming to salvation and to keep Christians from experiencing a devotion to God and a life of godliness.

His strategy is also to draw your attention elsewhere, to get you to dethrone Christ from ruling this planet. Have you heard the phrase, "Save the planet?" Who is king over planet Earth? Christ Jesus is. He doesn't need us to save the planet. We are to be responsible stewards of God's gift. But if you have taken that on as your mantra, you are making the devil smile.

So as Paul described the armor of God, using the image of a Roman soldier fully prepared for battle, every piece protects the believer from the lies of the devil. All of it is based on the truth about who Jesus Christ is, who you are in Christ, and what you have been given in Christ.

You may have heard this section of Ephesians 6 taught all by itself. But it should never be taken out of context of the whole book of Ephesians.

All those things listed as the armor of God come in one bundle with the rest of those spiritual blessing jewels we discovered in Ephesians 1:3-14. We got those because we are in Christ. Protection comes from what God has already provided. As Ephesians 6:10 says, "Be strong in the Lord and in His mighty power." Once we do that, what's next?

Verse 11 says to take your stand. Verse 13 says to stand your ground. Verse 14 says to stand firm. Against what? Verse 16 says to extinguish the flaming arrows of the evil one.

Remember that I said earlier that spiritual warfare is primarily waged over truth and error. The battleground is your mind. The flaming arrows are lies that are aimed at any weaknesses you have, any insecurities or fears. The result is to make you lose confidence in God and tempt you to go to substitutes that promise to work better for you.

Settling for less when you lose confidence in God

In the podcast for lesson 1, I shared with you what happens when we as believers lose confidence in our God alone to meet our needs. We turn to other power sources, substitutes that "seem to work." Doing this, we settle for less. Here are two popular traditions that become substitutes for Christ:

> **The legend of St. Joe substitute:** Bury a St. Joseph statue upside down near your for-sale sign to get your house sold quickly.

> **The prayer of St. Anthony substitute:** Pray a special prayer to someone called St. Anthony because he was good at finding lost things.

Traditions like that are probably more common than we think. Sometimes we do things without even thinking about why or what impact they have on our faith. But placing our faith in some ordinary man who died hundreds of years ago or believing there is power associated with his statue is not depending on the power of God. I believe when we do that kind of thing, we are settling for a substitute.

Isn't the most powerful God in the universe good enough for us? The One who wants us to know Him intimately and completely fills us with everything we need for successful life, isn't He good enough?

No one who ever lived or is alive today is closer to your Father God than you are. You are in Christ, seated with Him in heaven alongside God the Father, the closest you can be to the mightiest power in the universe. Why would you go elsewhere?

It is not that hard to get caught up in superstitious behavior without realizing it when you try something someone recommends for "quicker action from God," and it "seems to work." This "seems to work" outcome could be a flaming arrow from our enemy. Satan could be using your tendency to superstition (and impatience!) to get you away from a life of dependence on Christ. Could that be why some things "seem to work"?

Paul said that Satan masquerades as an angel of light (2 Corinthians 11:14). Making these substitutes "work" could be one way. It certainly makes Christians depend less on Jesus Christ's power on their behalf and replace Him with a power substitute—even one that is supposedly including God.

When we want something so badly we can taste it, that's when we are tempted to turn to substitutes the world recommends that seem to work, even religious substitutes. There are so many things out there to try. We go for the latest thing that guarantees success. Those are the flaming arrows of the enemy.

Don't do it! Don't seek the substitutes!

Stand firm in the treasure of victory in Christ.

Be strong **in the Lord**. You should not settle for less than what God Almighty offers you. You can put on all that our God has given to you and stand firm against any spiritual challenge.

Christ is more powerful than any substitute you could trust instead of Him. You can trust His power to protect you, to sell your house, to find your lost wallet, and to bring good into your life. He is greater than diplomas, social status, gazillions of dollars, lucky socks, formulas, saintly statues, and your own self-reliance.

There may be evil spiritual forces behind the people, the habits, and the situations that are messing up your life. But the answer is not to try out everything available to see if something sticks. You don't need substitute power. **The treasure you have in Jesus Christ is more powerful and valuable than anything you could substitute for Him**.

Believe that in your head and in your heart. Get rid of anything else you might be relying upon for spiritual power. Trust in what you already have in Jesus. Stand firm in that power.

Let Jesus satisfy your heart with the confidence that the treasure you have in Him is more powerful and valuable than anything you could substitute for Him.

Reflect

Ask God to help you recognize any areas of your life where you have accepted substitutes for Christ's power in your life.

Consider the specific ways and times He has given you victory over the "flaming arrows of the evil one" coming against you to deceive you and draw you into despair and hopelessness rather than confidence in Christ. What did He do?

Pray: Thank God for the treasure He has given you in Jesus Christ. Ask Him to help you recognize anything that you are substituting for Him. Ask Him to help you trust in Him alone for the power to be "successful" in life. Thank God for His incomparably great power working for you and within you.

The Biblical Process for Dealing with Recognized Sin

1. View yourself rightly.

Your identity is not "_____" (coveter, greedy, gossiper, whatever that sin is). You are in Christ, a child of God, who sometimes "_____" (covets, is greedy, gossips, etc.).

2. Agree with God (confess) that you are guilty of that behavior.

To **confess** biblically means *to agree with God about what you and He both know to be true.* Confession is not a formula, a process, or dependent on a mediator. Regarding sin in your life, it is not saying, "I'm sorry." It is saying, "I agree with you, God. I blew it!" You see your sin as something awful! Your sin is already forgiven.

3. Choose obedience (repentance).

Repentance means *to change your mind about that sin, to mourn its ugliness, resulting in changing your actions.* It's saying, "I recognize what I am doing is wrong. This fills me with sorrow because it displeases you, God. Please help me to live differently." Decide you want to live by the Spirit's power in that area of your life.

4. Depend on the Spirit's power by saying,

Our Lord Jesus Christ is not interested in our compliance or outward conformity as much as He desires our obedience from the heart. Consider saying, *"Lord Jesus, I can't do this, but you can do this in my life. I trust your Spirit to do this in me."* Depend on the Holy Spirit inside you for that change to take place, whatever it is. Then, watch what He does!

The Holy Spirit's Empowering Presence

We cannot see the Holy Spirit inside of us. But we know he is working inside us because we become aware of the evidence. These are some of the things the Spirit does for us:

> ➤ **He helps us understand what the Bible teaches.** Has someone explained something to you about the Bible, and you understood what she was saying? That's the Spirit inside of you helping you to understand. *John 16:13; 1 Cor. 2:13*

> ➤ **He gives us the words to tell others about Jesus and say that Jesus is God.** Have you wanted to tell someone about Jesus but didn't know what to say, then all of a sudden, the words just popped into your head for you to tell that person about Jesus? That's the Holy Spirit living inside of you prompting you with the right words to say. *John 14:26; 1 Corinthians 12:3*

> ➤ **He gives us assurance that we are God's children.** Have you ever felt really loved by God? That's the Spirit inside of you letting you know for sure that you are God's child, and He loves you. *Romans 8:16*

> ➤ **He makes us want to do what pleases God.** Do you have a desire to please God with your life? That's the Holy Spirit inside of you giving you that desire. *Romans 12:11; Jer. 33:31,33*

> ➤ **He helps us to feel joy as we serve Jesus and when we do the right things.** Have you ever felt really good when you chose to do the right thing or chose to be helpful? That's the Holy Spirit inside of you letting you feel God's pleasure. *Romans 14:17-18*

> ➤ **He makes us not want to do what doesn't please God.** Have you ever felt something tugging at you inside when you were tempted to do something wrong? That's the Holy Spirit living inside of you nudging you, reminding you what doesn't please God so you can choose not to do that. We can ask him to let us know in our thinking or feelings when we are tempted to do something bad. He promises to do that. *Galatians 5:16*

➢ **He makes us to become more like Jesus, especially in loving other people.** Have you ever started loving someone even more after you started praying for him/her? That's the Holy Spirit living inside of you doing that. *Galatians 5:22-23*

➢ **He makes us want to sing praises to God, in our hearts and out loud, and be thankful for God's goodness.** Do you like to sing praises to God? Do you feel thankful to God for his goodness to you? That's the Spirit living inside of you filling your heart with praise and thanksgiving to God. *Ephesians 5:18-20*

➢ **He prays for us when we need help or don't know how to pray.** Have you ever had a huge problem and didn't know what to ask God to do about it, but God took care of the problem anyway? That's the Holy Spirit living inside of you working to take care of your need before you even ask. *Romans 8:26-27*

Which of the above evidences have you recognized in your life?

Prayer: Thank God for specific ways and times his Spirit has worked in your life. Ask Him to make you more aware of His empowering presence in you.

Sources

The following resources were used in the preparation and writing of this study.

1. "A Saintly Hand Selling Your Home," *Dallas Morning News,* August 28, 2008

2. Clinton E. Arnold, *Power and Magic: the Concept of Power in Ephesians*

3. *Dr. Tom Constable's Notes on Ephesians, 2020 Edition*

4. *Dr. Tom Constable's Notes on Acts, 2020 Edition*

5. *Dr. Tom Constable's Notes on Daniel, 2020 Edition*

6. Oswald Chambers

7. *The NIV Study Bible New International Version,* Zondervan Bible Publishers, 1985.

8. Tim Stevenson, "Some Things to Remember about Spiritual Warfare"